Coping With Chronic Illness

✓Treatments *That Work*™

Coping With Chronic Illness

A COGNITIVE-BEHAVIORAL THERAPY APPROACH FOR ADHERENCE AND DEPRESSION

Therapist Guide

Steven A. Safren • Jeffrey S. Gonzalez • Nafisseh Soroudi

UNIVERSITY PRESS

2008

OXFORD
UNIVERSITY PRESS

Oxford University Press, Inc., publishes works that further
Oxford University's objective of excellence
in research, scholarship, and education.

Oxford   New York
Auckland   Cape Town   Dar es Salaam   Hong Kong   Karachi
Kuala Lumpur   Madrid   Melbourne   Mexico City   Nairobi
New Delhi   Shanghai   Taipei   Toronto

With offices in
Argentina   Austria   Brazil   Chile   Czech Republic   France   Greece
Guatemala   Hungary   Italy   Japan   Poland   Portugal   Singapore
South Korea   Switzerland   Thailand   Turkey   Ukraine   Vietnam

Copyright © 2008 by Oxford University Press, Inc.

Published by Oxford University Press, Inc.
198 Madison Avenue, New York, New York 10016

www.oup.com

Oxford is a registered trademark of Oxford University Press

ISBN 978-0-19-531516-5 (pbk.)

9 8 7 6 5 4 3 2 1

Printed in the United States of America
on acid-free paper

About Treatments *ThatWork*™

Stunning developments in health care have taken place over the past several years, but many of our widely accepted interventions and strategies in mental health and behavioral medicine have been brought into question by research evidence as not only lacking benefit but perhaps inducing harm. Other strategies have been proven effective using the best current standards of evidence, resulting in broad-based recommendations to make these practices more available to the public. Several recent developments are behind this revolution. First, we have arrived at a much deeper understanding of pathology, both psychological and physical, which has led to the development of new, more precisely targeted interventions. Second, our research methodologies have improved substantially, such that we have reduced threats to internal and external validity, making the outcomes more directly applicable to clinical situations. Third, governments around the world and health care systems and policy makers have decided that the quality of care should improve, that it should be evidence based, and that it is in the public's interest to ensure that this happens (Barlow, 2004; Institute of Medicine, 2001).

Of course, the major stumbling block for clinicians everywhere is the accessibility of newly developed evidence-based psychological interventions. Workshops and books can go only so far in acquainting responsible and conscientious practitioners with the latest behavioral health care practices and their applicability to individual patients. This new series, Treatments *ThatWork*™, is devoted to communicating these exciting new interventions to clinicians on the frontlines of practice.

The manuals and workbooks in this series contain step-by-step detailed procedures for assessing and treating specific problems and diagnoses. But this series also goes beyond the books and manuals by providing ancillary materials that will approximate the supervisory process in assisting practitioners in the implementation of these procedures in their practice.

In our emerging health care system, the growing consensus is that evidence-based practice offers the most responsible course of action for the mental health professional. All behavioral health care clinicians deeply desire to provide the best possible care for their patients. In this series, our aim is to close the dissemination and information gap and make that possible.

This therapist guide and the companion workbook for clients describe a cognitive-behavioral treatment (CBT) that targets both depression and adherence in individuals living with chronic illnesses who are also depressed. Depression is common among individuals with chronic medical conditions and can significantly impair their ability to manage their illnesses. Depressed individuals tend to practice poor self-care behaviors, which may include forgetting to take their medication as directed (or not taking it all), missing medical appointments, and neglecting to exercise and eat healthfully. Increasing engagement in these sorts of behaviors is the focus of this modular program. The treatment is based on standard interventions used in CBT for depression but chosen and adapted for persons with chronic illness, with the specific emphasis on self-care behaviors and medical adherence. Clients will learn core skills such as problem solving and cognitive restructuring in order to help them take better care of themselves. They will also learn relaxation and breathing techniques to help them cope with symptoms and side effects. Complete with step-by-step instructions for delivering this unique intervention, this book is sure to become an invaluable resource for mental health professionals and their chronically ill clients.

David H. Barlow, Editor-in-Chief,
Treatments *ThatWork*™
Boston, Massachusetts

References

Barlow, D. H. (2004). Psychological treatments. *American Psychologist, 59*, 869–878.

Institute of Medicine. (2001). *Crossing the quality chasm: A new health system for the 21st century*. Washington, DC: National Academy Press.

Contents

Figures and Worksheets

Chapter 1   *Introductory Information for Therapists*

Background Information and Purpose of This Program

This treatment manual and the accompanying client workbook describe a cognitive-behavioral treatment that targets both depression and adherence in individuals living with both a chronic illness and depression. For the purposes of this guide, we will refer to the treatment program as CBT-AD (cognitive-behavioral therapy for adherence and depression).

Depression is prevalent among individuals with chronic medical conditions and can significantly impair their ability to manage their illness. Patients with both a chronic medical condition and depression experience greater distress and worse medical outcomes (including mortality) than do those with a medical condition who do not have depression. Although there is some emerging evidence that depression can impact illness directly through associated biochemical changes, one of the reasons for worse medical outcomes in individuals with depression is that depression may contribute to poor self-care behaviors, including medical nonadherence.

Individuals with chronic illness and depression represent a complex population with heterogeneous individual needs. To address those needs, this manual is designed in a modular format. Each module of treatment is based on standard interventions used in cognitive-behavioral therapy (CBT) for depression but chosen and adapted for persons with chronic illness, with an emphasis on self-care behaviors and medical adherence. Because of the complexity of managing a medical illness comorbid with depression and simultaneously increasing adherence, therapist flexibility is key. For example, therapist flexibility may be necessary in regard to the delivery of specific modules based on individual need, as well as the sequencing of the modules (though we recommend that the psychoeducation module come first). It is also likely that the number of sessions per module will vary according to the clinical presentation and needs of the client. Additionally, individuals with a chronic illness and depression frequently experience multiple significant life stressors. Therapist flexibility is necessary to balance the need to set and adhere to an agenda in order to teach the coping skills described in this manual with the need to provide necessary psychosocial support to clients when stressful life events occur.

Problem Focus: Depression and Adherence in Chronic Illness

Mental health professionals who treat depression are likely to encounter clients who have comorbid chronic medical conditions. Some data suggest that up to 30% of individuals with a medical condition experience depression and that depression is the most common condition that co-occurs with a medical illness. Research in various illnesses, including HIV (e.g., Dew et al., 1997; Rabkin, 1996), diabetes (e.g., Anderson, Freedland, Clouse, & Lustman, 2001; Egede, Zheng, & Simpson, 2002), heart disease (e.g., Januzzi, Stern, Pasternak, & DeSantis, 2000; Frasure-Smith, Lesperance, & Talajic, 1995b), cancer (e.g., Spiegel & Giese-Davis, 2003; Pirl & Roth, 1999), stroke (e.g., Morris, Robinson, Andrzejewski, Samuels, & Price, 1993), and life-threatening illness in general (Silverstone, 1990), shows higher prevalence rates of depression. Rates of depression in patients with comorbid medical illnesses increase 2–5% in community settings, 5–10% in primary care, and 6–14% or greater in patients with comorbid medical illness (Katon & Ciechanowski, 2002; Wells et al., 1991; Katon & Sullivan, 1990).

Why Do Depression and Chronic Medical Illness Overlap?

There are many potential reasons for the overlap between depression and chronic illness. Living with a chronic illness can be stressful and can limit one's involvement in pleasurable activities. Physical symptoms such as fatigue can impair one's ability to maintain one's usual activities and can cause losses in functioning. Adjusting to an illness that has waxing and waning symptoms can also be upsetting. Finally, cognitive aspects may include perceptions of loss of control or altered goals in life. These factors together can result in distress and/or depression.

In some cases, the relationship between depression and chronic illness may even be cyclical. In diabetes, for example, depressive symptoms such as reduced energy, lower motivation, and difficulties with problem solving negatively impact self-treatment and can lead to hyperglycemia or high blood sugar. In turn, hyperglycemia and the threat of complications can lead to hopelessness, self-blame, and helplessness. In HIV, depression can lead to worse immune functioning, both through worse treatment adherence and possibly through reduced levels of the hormone cortisol. This hormone is produced by the adrenal glands and helps regulate blood pressure and cardiovascular function, as well as the body's use of proteins, carbohydrates, and fats (Antoni et al., 2005). Having worse immune functioning leaves one at risk for various infections, causing symptoms and impairment, and consequently leading back to increased depression. Thus clients with chronic illness and depression may experience a vicious cycle of increasing depression and worsening illness and may require interventions aimed at both decreasing depression *and* improving self-care.

Depression Comorbid With a Chronic Illness Is Costly and Impairing

Depression is quite costly in the context of chronic medical conditions. In diabetes, for example, patients with depression fill nearly twice as many prescriptions, make twice as many ambulatory care visits, and have total health care expenditures 4.5 times greater than patients with diabetes and no depression (Egede et al., 2002). Rates of functional disability are considerably higher in individuals with comorbid depression and diabetes (77.8%) when compared with individuals with depression without diabetes (51.3%), with diabetes without depression (58.1%), or with neither depression nor diabetes (24.5%; Egede, 2004). In diabetes, depression results in significant functional impairments, reductions in quality of life, and increased disabilities (Bruce, Davis, & Davis, 2005; Goldney, Phillips, Fisher, & Wilson, 2004) and more than doubles the risk for mortality (Katon et al., 2005).

Depression is associated with increased mortality rates, both in the context of chronic illness and in community samples (e.g., Cuijpers & Schoevers, 2004). Decreased adherence to treatment has been proposed as one of the likely mechanisms through which depression confers an impact on mortality outcomes in the context of chronic illness.

Depression Affects Adherence to Medical and Self-Care Behaviors

Individuals with depression are three times more likely than nondepressed individuals to be nonadherent with medical treatment recommendations (DiMatteo, Lepper, & Croghan, 2000). A strong body of evidence supports the association between depression and treatment nonadherence in chronic illness populations, including individuals who are post-myocardial infarction (Ziegelstein et al., 2000) and in cancer patients in chemotherapy (Valente, Saunders, & Cohen, 1994). Studies from our group (Gonzalez et al., 2004; Safren et al., 2001) and others (e.g., Singh et al., 1996; Simoni, Frick, Lockhart, & Liebovitz, 2002) demonstrate that, in HIV, higher levels of depression are associated with worse adherence to HIV medications. These findings suggest a robust relationship between depression and poor adherence and point to the need for interventions to enhance adherence in individuals with depression and physical illness.

Depression May Be Hidden in Individuals With Chronic Illness

Depression goes undetected and likely untreated by the health care system in nearly half of comorbid patients. For example, among diabetic patients correctly recognized as depressed, 43% received one or more antidepressant prescriptions and less than 7% received four or more psychotherapy sessions during a 12-month period (Katon et al., 2004). Rodin, Nolan, and Katz (2005) suggest several possible reasons for the underdiagnosis and undertreatment of depression in the medical system, including the overlap of symptoms of depression and medical symptoms and the difficulty of differentiating sadness as a natural response to a serious diagnosis from clinical depression. However, depression in the context of medical illness is treatable—both with medications and with CBT. The present manual describes a CBT approach that involves treating depression *and* teaching skills to improve medical adherence.

Different Types of Depression: Diagnostic Criteria

In the following tables we list the criteria from the *Diagnostic and Statistical Manual of Mental Disorders* (*DSM-IV-TR;* American Psychiatric Association, 2000) for the most common types of depression, including major depression, dysthymia, and bipolar disorder, which has features of mania and depression. This treatment manual is mainly designed for individuals with unipolar depression. However, in our studies we included individuals with bipolar disorder who were currently depressed and who had not recently experienced a manic or hypomanic episode. We believe that this manual would be appropriate for those with bipolar depression if they were currently depressed. The presence of mania would necessitate other interventions to stabilize mood, which are not focused on in this manual. Also, although we have designed this treatment manual for use with clients who have symptoms of depression that are severe enough to warrant a clinical diagnosis, there is evidence that lower levels of depressive symptoms also negatively impact self-care and medication adherence (e.g., Gonzalez et al., in press), and it is likely that the strategies that we present in this manual could be modified for use with patients who have some symptoms of depression, even if they do not meet criteria for a formal diagnosis.

Major Depressive Disorder

Major depressive disorder is characterized by single or recurrent depressive episodes in the absence of manic or hypomanic symptoms. The specific criteria from the *DSM-IV-TR* (APA, 2000, p. 356) follow.

A. The person experiences a single major depressive episode:
   1. For a major depressive episode a person must have experienced at least five of the following nine symptoms during the same 2-week period or longer, for most of the time almost

every day, and this must represent a change from his or her prior level of functioning. One of the symptoms must be either (a) depressed mood or (b) loss of interest.

    a.   Depressed mood. For children and adolescents, this may be irritable mood.

    b.   A significantly reduced level of interest or pleasure in most or all activities.

    c.   A considerable loss or gain of weight (e.g., 5% or more change in weight in a month when not dieting). This may include an increase or decrease in appetite. Children may fail to show expected gains in weight.

    d.   Difficulty falling or staying asleep (insomnia) or sleeping more than usual (hypersomnia).

    e.   Behavior that is agitated or slowed down, which is observable by others.

    f.   Feeling fatigued or having diminished energy.

    g.   Thoughts of worthlessness or extreme guilt (though not about being ill).

    h.   Reduced ability to think, concentrate, or make decisions.

    i.   Frequent thoughts of death or suicide (with or without a specific plan), or attempt at suicide.

2.   The person's symptoms do not indicate a mixed episode.

3.   The person's symptoms are a cause of great distress or difficulty in functioning at home, work, or other important areas.

4.   The person's symptoms are not caused by substance use (e.g., alcohol, drugs, medication) or a medical disorder.

5.   The person's symptoms are not due to normal grief or bereavement over the death of a loved one, they continue for more than 2 months, or they include great difficulty in functioning, frequent thoughts of worthlessness, thoughts of suicide, symptoms that are psychotic, or behavior that is slowed down (psychomotor retardation).

B. Another disorder does not better explain the major depressive episode.

C. The person has never had a manic, mixed, or a hypomanic episode (unless an episode was due to a medical disorder or use of a substance).

Dysthymic Disorder

Dysthymic disorder is characterized by chronic, persistent low-level depressive symptoms over a longer period of time. The specific criteria from the *DSM-IV-TR* (APA, 2000, pp. 380–381) are listed here.

A. A person has depressed mood for most the time almost every day for at least 2 years. Children and adolescents may have irritable mood, and the time frame is at least 1 year.

B. While depressed, a person experiences at least two of the following symptoms:
   1. Either overeating or lack of appetite.
   2. Sleeping too much or having difficulty sleeping.
   3. Fatigue or lack of energy.
   4. Poor self-esteem.
   5. Difficulty with concentration or decision making.
   6. Feeling hopeless.

C. A person has not been free of the symptoms during the 2-year time period (1 year for children and adolescents) for more than 2 months at a time.

D. During the 2-year time period (1 year for children and adolescents) there has not been a major depressive episode.

E. A person has not had a manic, mixed, or hypomanic episode.

F. The symptoms are not present only during the course of another chronic disorder.

G. A medical condition or the use of substances (i.e., alcohol, drugs, medication, toxins) does not cause the symptoms.

H. The person's symptoms are a cause of great distress or difficulty in functioning at home, work, or other important areas.

Bipolar Spectrum Disorders

The bipolar spectrum mood disorders (i.e., bipolar I, bipolar II, cyclothymia) are differentiated from unipolar depressive disorders in that individuals also experience hypomanic or manic episodes. The word *bipolar* is used because individuals experience two emotional extremes—depressed mood at times and at other times excessive euphoria. Individuals with bipolar I experience full manic episodes; those with bipolar II experience hypomanic episodes—episodes that are not as severe as manic episodes; and those with cyclothymia experience a mix of low-level depressive episodes and hypomanic episodes. Again, we believe this manual is relevant for individuals with bipolar disorder only if they are not currently experiencing manic or hypomanic episodes and if this aspect of their disorder is stabilized.

Development of This Treatment Program and Evidence Base

The empirical basis of this approach comes from several sources. First, there are many treatment studies for depression in nonmedical populations that demonstrate the efficacy of CBT. Second, there are emerging studies of CBT approaches for depression in the context of medical conditions, and these studies have demonstrated evidence for the efficacy of CBT in these patients, particularly those with HIV or diabetes. Third, the empirical base is supported by our research on a cognitive-behavioral adherence intervention (now module 2 in this manual), which was shown to successfully improve medication adherence in patients with HIV. Finally, we have completed one randomized controlled trial and two open-phase case-series studies of the specific intervention described in this manual, targeting individuals with HIV and depression. At the time of writing, we are conducting ongoing evaluations of this approach in HIV and diabetes in two separate randomized controlled trials sponsored by the National Institutes of Health.

Studies of CBT for Depression

Over 30 years of research has consistently validated CBT as an efficacious treatment for depression, with many studies showing effects similar to or greater than those for medications (see Dobson, 1989; Robinson, Berman, & Neimeyer, 1990, for reviews and meta-analyses). CBT has also been shown to have additive effects for residual symptoms of depression not fully treated by antidepressants (see Deckersbach, Berman, & Neimeyer, 2000; Otto, Pava, & Sprich-Buckminster, 1996).

CBT for depression also generally shows lower relapse rates than pharmacotherapy (Blackburn, Eunson, & Bishop, 1986; McLean & Hakstian, 1990; Simons, Murphy, Levine, & Wetzel, 1986), and the protection against relapse for clients treated with CBT extends to those who began with pharmacotherapy alone (Evans et al., 1992; Fava et al., 1995; Fava et al., 1996; Fava, Rafanelli, Grandi, Canestrari, & Morphy, 1998; Paykel et al., 1999; Simons et al., 1986; Teasdale et al., 2000). Fava, Rafanelli, Grandi, Conti, and Belluardo (1998), for example, compared CBT with clinical management alone in clients with chronic depression (three or more episodes) who were being treated with antidepressants. Eighty percent of those with clinical management of medications alone relapsed over the 2-year assessment period, compared with only 25% of those who received CBT and clinical management of medications.

CBT for Depression in Medical Illnesses That Require High Levels of Adherence

The approach described in the subsequent chapters of this manual integrates CBT for depression with adherence enhancement approaches. Others, however, have studied cognitive-behavioral therapy and cognitive-behavioral stress management for depression in the context of medical illness but did not specifically address adherence in the intervention. We recently reviewed this literature on HIV, focusing on randomized controlled trials (Olatunji, Mimiaga, O'Clereigh, & Safren, 2006), and found four studies that targeted depression directly and five studies that targeted distress and stress management. Accordingly, as shown in studies of CBT for depression in samples of individuals without medical illness, CBT for depression in HIV appears to be a useful, efficacious approach.

We also reviewed this literature on diabetes, another disease requiring high levels of adherence. Lustman, Griffith, Freedland, Kissel, and Clouse (1998) conducted a randomized controlled trial of CBT among 51 type 2 diabetics with major depression. In this study, all patients participated in a diabetes education program throughout the trial, but the CBT intervention did not specifically address diabetes self-care. Patients who were randomly assigned to receive CBT were compared with patients who only received education. Results showed that CBT did effectively reduce depression symptoms and that 85% of the treatment group reached depression remission on completion of the trial compared with 27% of controls ($p < .001$). At the 6-month follow-up, the remission rates for CBT and control participants were 33% and 70%, respectively ($p = .03$). Others have successfully applied CBT for depression to individuals with diabetes using a stepped-care approach whereby patients had increasing levels of intervention as needed (e.g., Katon et al., 2004; Williams et al., 2004).

Life-Steps: A Single-Session Adherence Intervention

The idea behind CBT-AD also stemmed from our previous randomized controlled trial of a "minimal" adherence intervention—a single-session adherence intervention that did not specifically address comorbid depression. This intervention targets a series of informational, problem-solving, and cognitive-behavioral steps needed to successfully adhere to HIV medications. The description of the intervention, presented in chapter 4, is also available as an article in the journal *Cognitive and Behavioral Practice* (Safren, Otto, & Worth, 1999). The results of the randomized controlled trial are described in detail by Safren et al. (2001).

At baseline (before delivering the intervention), we examined several correlates of adherence, which included depression, self-efficacy, punishment beliefs about HIV and HIV medications, and social support. All were significant at the bivariate level. When examining the unique variance for predictors of adherence, however, depression emerged as the only statistically significant predictor.

We then randomly assigned clients with adherence problems to either receive or not receive the adherence intervention. Participants in the randomized study were the 49 men and 7 women from the original sample who reported that they had not taken all of their prescribed HIV antiretrovirals in the preceding 2 weeks. The main outcome variable was self-report medication adherence scores for the preceding 2 weeks. After 2 weeks, those who received the intervention displayed statistically significantly greater changes in adherence scores from baseline to week 2, as compared with those who did not receive the intervention. Accordingly, at the 12-week follow-up, there was a statistically significant improvement in adherence from week 0 to week 12. There was no significant main effect, however, for condition, and the interaction of time and condition across groups was not significant.

These results generally suggest the potential utility of a brief adherence intervention. However, baseline depression in this sample was high, and depression interacted with intervention outcome. This led us to consider integrating CBT for depression with this intervention for adherence.

Specific Studies of CBT-AD in HIV Treatment

The full intervention described in this manual, cognitive behavioral therapy for adherence and depression (CBT-AD), has been studied in the context of one open-phase case-series study and one open-phase trial of individuals with HIV and depression who did not report active substance abuse. The randomized trial was funded by the National Institute of Mental Health (Grant No. MH066660). It is also being tested in an ongoing study funded by the National Institute on Drug Abuse (Grant No. DA018603), targeting individuals who are HIV-infected and receiving methadone maintenance. This project includes a completed case-series study and an ongoing randomized controlled trial.

Our first case series targeted men with HIV who were infected through sex with another man. Participants were five men, including an African American male in his mid-40s who was on disability, a white male in his early 30s who worked full time, a white male in his late 40s who was on disability, an African American male in his late 40s who worked part time and was on disability, and a white male in his early 50s with a relatively high socioeconomic status who worked full time. At baseline, all participants met criteria for major depressive disorder despite stable treatment with an antidepressant, and all reported problems adhering to their HIV medications. During the course of treatment, adherence to antiretroviral medications, as assessed by electronic pill cap ratings, increased, and depression, as assessed by the Beck Depression Inventory (BDI; Beck, Ward, Mendelson, Mock, & Erbaugh, 1961) decreased. One individual discontinued participation in treatment after four sessions but agreed to complete the posttreatment assessment. According to the Structured Clinical Interview for *DSM-IV*, only one of the five individuals presented still met current *DSM-IV* criteria for a major depressive episode at the end of the treatment. This individual, however, had a relatively low clinical global impression score (CGI; a 1–7 scale of depression severity; National Institute of Mental Health, 1985) for depression (3 = mildly ill) at posttreatment and a clinically significantly higher one at pretreatment (5 = markedly ill). All individuals made clinically significant improvements as evident by a drop in at least 2 CGI points from pretreatment to posttreatment.

Our first randomized controlled trial of CBT-AD is also now complete (Safren et al., 2006). In this study, patients with HIV and depression (major depression or bipolar with depression and no recent manic episode) were randomly assigned to either the full CBT-AD for HIV medication adherence and depression or to the single-session intervention for HIV medication adherence referred to earlier (module 1 of this manual; Safren et al., 1999; Safren et al., 2001). In both conditions, a letter was sent to the patients' primary care physicians describing their symptoms of depression and other psychiatric diagnoses in case the physicians wished to make additional referrals or make changes to prescribed psychiatric medications. This was a crossover design in that individuals assigned to the adherence intervention could cross over to the full CBT-AD intervention if they desired after the first outcome assessment. Participants were also seen for two follow-up assessments—at 3 months after completion of the intervention (approximately 6 months from randomization) and 12 months postrandomization. The primary adherence outcome was based on data from an electronic pill cap that indicated whether patients had opened their pill bottles at the appropriate times over the previous 2 weeks. The primary depression outcomes were Hamilton Depression Scale scores, as assessed by an independent assessor who was blind to treatment assignment, and the corresponding clinical global impression rating. Participants also completed the BDI.

Forty-two individuals (of the 45 that were randomized) completed the pre- and posttreatment assessments. Unlike those in many studies of CBT for depression, this sample evidenced significant psychiatric comorbidity. Of our 42 completers, 64% (*n* = 27) had at least one additional *DSM* diagnosis, and 38% (*n* = 16) had two additional *DSM* diagnoses.

Those who were assigned the full CBT-AD intervention showed significantly greater improvements in adherence and depression than the comparison condition at the posttreatment assessment, with large effect sizes. At the 3-month follow-up, individuals who received CBT-AD maintained their gains, and those who crossed over to CBT-AD also significantly improved from baseline. This pattern of results occurred for depression, as rated by an independent assessor who was blind to treatment assignment and in self-reported symptoms measured by the BDI. The adherence outcome was percent adherence within a 2-hour window of target time using the electronic pill caps.

Currently we are testing the applicability of this intervention in an even more complex population—individuals with HIV and depression who are receiving methadone maintenance for opioid dependence. We have completed an open-phase trial and have a full-scale efficacy study under way. The open trial included five HIV-infected individuals (four women, one man) receiving methadone treatment for heroin dependence (Soroudi et al., in press). This open-phase trial also revealed clinically significant improvements in adherence and depression. These were evidenced as both gradual improvements in depression, as measured by weekly self-report inventories (BDI), and gradual improvements in adherence, as measured by the electronic pill caps and pre- and postclinical assessments.

Finally, we are currently testing the intervention in individuals with type 2 diabetes and depression in a two-arm randomized controlled trial. We hypothesize that participants who receive the CBT-AD intervention will show greater improvements in both depression and diabetes self-care behaviors as compared with controls, and we expect that these changes will result in better control of diabetes.

Conceptual Basis of CBT-AD

Cognitive-behavioral therapy for adherence and depression is based on the model depicted in figure 1.1. Accordingly, symptoms of depression (e.g., low concentration, loss of interest, suicidality) and associated problems (e.g., difficulty with problem solving, low motivation) can interfere with the behaviors needed to adhere to a medical regimen. In the

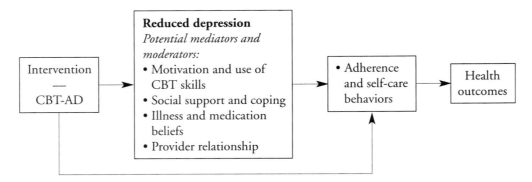

Figure 1.1.

Cognitive-Behavioral Model of Depression and Adherence

context of chronic illness, illness symptoms can also contribute to symptoms of depression, and vice versa. Hence, our model posits that by treating depression with a skills-based psychosocial approach, we can help individuals adhere to their medical regimens and therefore have improved psychosocial and medical outcomes.

Risks and Benefits of This Treatment Program

As this is a psychosocial behavioral treatment, there are no known medical risks in participating in this program. Cognitive-behavioral therapy is a directive, skills-based treatment. There is always the risk that it will not work. In this case, clients may feel sad, upset, or even hopeless about their continued symptoms of depression. Therapists are encouraged to discuss this risk with clients and plan for exploring reasons for potential treatment nonresponse. As with any treatment of depression, therapists should also actively monitor suicidality and be prepared to refer for additional, more intensive treatment (e.g., partial inpatient or inpatient, psychopharmacological consultation, augmentation, or change) when needed.

There are many potential benefits to the treatment program. Depression is a distressing, disabling, and interfering condition. In and of itself, depression can significantly impact one's overall quality of life. This treatment program targets both depression and adherence to one's health regimen. Specific symptoms of depression (poor concentration, loss of interest) or associated symptoms (low motivation, poor problem solving) can certainly interfere with one's ability to adhere to a regimen of treatment for a chronic illness. In HIV, adherence to medications is critical for treatment success. In diabetes, adherence to glucose monitoring, insulin, and medications can prevent further complications and morbidity. Many other medical illnesses require strict adherence to the regimens, and the approach used in this manual may be applicable to a wide range of self-care regimens, particularly when the chronic illness is comorbid with depression.

Alternative Treatments

As far as we know, CBT-AD as described in this manual is the only psychosocial intervention that integrates the treatment of depression with a psychosocial approach to increasing adherence. An alternative psychosocial treatment for depression which has been demonstrated as efficacious is interpersonal psychotherapy (IPT; Weissman, 2005). Also, antidepressant medications have been validated as treatments for depression. These alternatives should be discussed with clients.

The Role of Medications

There are a variety of psychopharmacological agents available for the treatment of depression, with efficacy demonstrated in many randomized controlled trials (see Sadock & Sadock, 2003). CBT-AD, as described in this manual and as tested empirically, is designed to treat depression, either in individuals on antidepressant medications who still show symptoms or in individuals who are not currently on antidepressant medications. Having an approach for those who are already on medications is important, because, although medications do work, only 50% of those who are treated with antidepressants alone are considered treatment responders (e.g., Agency for Health Care Policy and Research Depression Guideline Panel [AHCPR], 1993a,b; Fava, Alpert, Nierenberg, Worthington, & Rosenbaum, 2000; Fava & Davidson, 1996), and of those who do respond, only 50–65% attain complete remission. This leaves significant symptoms that could be addressed with a psychosocial skills-based approach. Our studies of CBT-AD have begun after stabilization on medications so that we can determine the degree to which improvements from the treatment occur over and above the effects of medications.

Outline of This Treatment Program

The main modules for CBT-AD are (1) psychoeducation and motivational interviewing regarding treating depression and being adherent to one's medical regimen; (2) adherence training; (3) activity scheduling; (4) cognitive restructuring; (5) problem solving; (6) relaxation training/ diaphragmatic breathing; and (7) review, maintenance, and relapse prevention. The treatment follows a modular approach so that core CBT skills can be learned, followed by focused work on problems specific to the individual. To maximize the balance between providing support to clients and also teaching new skills, we recommend that the format of every session begin with a mood check (we provide the Center for Epidemiologic Studies Depression Scale; CES-D), a review of adherence and of homework and ongoing progress from previous modules, and setting an agenda for the session. This should be done at the start of every session, regardless of whether it is a new module or a continuation of a module. We also recommend that therapists be flexible with clients in terms of the order of the modules, the amount of time spent on any one module, and the application of emergent client problems to the specific modules of treatment. This modular approach helps to make the treatment more relevant for each client and allows a more flexible sequence in the delivery of interventions based on the client's presenting issues.

Each module builds on previous modules, and each session begins with an assessment and discussion of depression and adherence for the previous week. The course of treatment is designed to be similar to a standardized cognitive-behavioral therapy, but though clients learn core CBT skills (cognitive restructuring and activity scheduling), active training in problem solving and relaxation are also implemented. The problem-solving techniques complement the skills training for adherence. Because problem-solving skills can be impaired as a result of depression and because effective problem-solving skills are important for the management of medical illness, it is essential to directly teach these skills. Finally, we teach applied relaxation and slow breathing to help patients cope with side effects of medications, illness-related symptoms, or pain. These relaxation exercises can also improve sleep hygiene and stress management.

Use of the Workbook

The client workbook is meant to be an accompaniment to this therapist manual. As discussed, flexibility is required in terms of the number of sessions spent on individual modules. Hence, the therapist manual and the client workbook are not set up on a session-by-session basis. Instead, we provide text to describe the entire module, keeping in mind that some modules may take several sessions.

We include the CES-D in the client workbook as the measure of depression to be completed each week. This measure is in the public domain and can be a reliable way to track progress. It is important, however, to remind clients to complete this measure regarding their mood since the previous session. We recommend that sessions be weekly; hence this time period would correspond to the previous week, in accordance with the wording of the CES-D.

Other forms in the manual include a sample worksheet for the adherence intervention, worksheets for mood and adherence monitoring, problem solving, and cognitive restructuring, and an activity checklist. The materials for cognitive restructuring include client instructions, as well as forms for identifying negative thinking and formulating rational responses.

Chapter 2 · *Overview of Adherence Behaviors for Selected Illnesses*

Most medical illnesses require treatment adherence behaviors. Although HIV/AIDS and diabetes may be more widely known regarding the importance of strict adherence, health conditions such as hypertension or high blood pressure, asthma, cardiac disease, and organ transplant also contain aspects of the treatment that rely heavily on patient self-care behaviors and/or behavioral change. However, as articulated throughout this manual, symptoms of depression can have a strong impact on the motivation and skills needed to maintain strict adherence.

The first client session of this treatment approach focuses on psychoeducation and motivational interviewing regarding CBT for depression and adherence. The next module, called "Life-Steps" is dedicated to adherence skills training. The remaining modules then integrate CBT for adherence with CBT for depression. As an aid for clinicians who may be unfamiliar with particular medical illnesses, we present in this chapter a basic overview of two of the most common health conditions that require high levels of adherence/self-care behaviors, HIV/AIDS and diabetes, and the particular adherence behaviors that accompany each condition. We then provide information on additional diseases for which this approach may be useful. This can serve as important background information for the Life-Steps module and for the material that integrates CBT for depression with adherence training.

HIV/AIDS

Currently, the treatment for HIV/AIDS is highly active antiretroviral therapy, or HAART. HAART is perhaps the most rigorous, demanding, and unforgiving of any outpatient oral treatment ever introduced. Almost perfect adherence to HAART is required to maximize the chances of treatment success and to minimize the chances of developing medication resistance. This is difficult for patients because many experience immediate and long-term side effects, including fatigue, nausea, diarrhea, insomnia, abnormal fat accumulation, taste alterations, and peripheral neuropathy (damage to the peripheral nervous system; Ammassari et al., 2001; Chesney, Morin, & Sherr, 2000). Additionally, HAART needs to be taken in the long term—indefinitely. In contrast, in other diseases (e.g., hypertension), chronically administered drug therapies are tolerant of mild to moderate nonadherence because they do not require continuous therapeutic coverage and may have a long duration of effect after dosing. Full therapeutic benefit of HAART may require not only administration of a high proportion of total doses, as in other chronic illness treatments, but strict and near perfect attention to dosing frequency, timing, and food requirements.

For HIV, the main area of adherence that this manual addresses is adherence to medications, or HAART.

Key Terms

- **HIV:** Human-immunodeficiency virus. This virus is recognized as the cause of AIDS.

- **Viral Load or Viral Burden:** The amount of HIV virus that a person with HIV has in his or her blood. Usually this is the number of copies per milliliter of blood plasma. Usually less than 50ml is considered "**undetectable**" or "**suppressed**" in that standard devices do not detect this level of virus. Sometimes less than 75ml or less than 400ml is considered undetectable. The goal of HAART is to get a patient to a "suppressed" or "undetectable" level.

- **CD4 (or T-cell):** These immune system cells protect the body from viral, fungal, and other infections. HIV attacks these cells, and their destruction leaves the body susceptible to infections that they might not otherwise acquire. Because of a low CD4 or T-cell count, infections have the opportunity to infect a person with HIV. These infections, which a person would normally not get, are called "opportunistic" infections.

- **AIDS:** Acquired immunodeficiency syndrome. This is the more severe manifestation of HIV. According to the CDC, a person is considered to have AIDS when his or her CD4 count is under 200 or he or she has certain opportunistic infections.

- **Resistance:** HIV replicates quickly. During this rapid replication, errors are frequent and can result in mutations of the virus strain. If these mutations are of a form that is not responsive to medications, a person is said to have "resistance."

- **HAART:** Highly active antiretroviral therapy. The treatment regimens that attack HIV. This usually consists of at least three different medications, coming from the following classes: protease inhibitors (e.g., ritonavir/Norvir, indinavir/Crixivan, saquinavir/Invirase), NRTIs—nucleoside reverse transcriptase inhibitors (e.g., AZT, ddI, 3TC), and NNRTIs—non-nucleoside reverse transcriptase inhibitors (e.g. delavirdine/Rescriptor, efavirenz/Sustiva, nevirapine/Viramune).

HIV as a Chronic Illness

Recent advances in the treatment of the human immunodeficiency virus (HIV) have increased the life expectancy and quality of life for HIV-infected individuals, transforming HIV in the United States from a "death sentence" to a manageable chronic illness. This mainly came with the introduction of HAART. Although not a cure, combination drug therapies that began to be developed and tested in the mid-1990s represented a major breakthrough in the treatment of HIV. Clinical trials showed that combinations of highly active antiretroviral therapies, commonly referred to as "drug cocktails," could substantially reduce the levels of HIV in the bloodstream. This reduction in the immune system "viral load," in turn, was shown to lead to improved immune system functioning, reduced frequency of opportunistic infections, and lower rates of viral mutation. These changes resulted in a dramatic slowing of the progression of the disease for many patients.

The New Era of HIV Management

In the United States and other countries where HAART is readily available to patients, many people are now living with HIV infection for many years—even indefinitely if there are not other complications. Although treatment advances have increased the life expectancy of HIV-infected patients, the medications also demand near perfect adherence to achieve maximum benefit and avoid treatment failure. Maintaining excellent patient adherence remains an important challenge in the control of the virus and provides a decisive opportunity for behavioral health clinicians to improve the health and quality of life of HIV-infected patients.

Although initial research showed that HAART was quite successful in improving immune system functioning and outcomes for HIV-infected patients, these effects have been difficult to attain in clinical practice. In clinical trials, various regimens of HAART have been shown to successfully suppress viral load in 60–90% of patients (Carpenter et al., 1997). These high percentages were demonstrated in the optimal setting of clinical trials (efficacy) with research participants who had not previously been treated for HIV. However, these rates cannot easily be duplicated in real-world clinical practice (effectiveness). In fact, only 50% of clinical practice patients are likely to achieve successful viral control when given the same HAART regimens tested in clinical trials research (Fätkenheuer et al., 1997; Casado et al., 1998). This difference between efficacy and effectiveness may be due to differences between the usually highly circumscribed samples in clinical trials and the much more complex clinical population of HIV-infected individuals.

The Importance of Adherence in the Era of HAART

If HAART is highly potent and adherence is perfect, viral replication is theoretically shut off, and resistant mutations do not arise. However, the clinical reality is that most patients are less than perfect in their level of adherence and consequently achieve incomplete antiretroviral potency. The high rate of error-prone HIV replication places HIV-infected individuals on HAART at risk for viral replication of medication-resistant strains. Although HAART is a highly potent treatment, perfect or near perfect adherence to HAART is necessary in order to prevent breakthrough of resistant strains of the virus. Not only does this represent a serious consequence for individuals taking HAART, but it is also a major public health concern, as it is possible for these drug-resistant strains of HIV to be transmitted from one person to another.

How Much Adherence Is Enough?

Even modest or occasional nonadherence to HAART greatly diminishes the benefits of treatment. Whereas the general adherence literature in other chronic illnesses has generally considered 80% adherence to be adequate, research on the relationship between viral load and adherence to HAART suggests that much higher levels of adherence need to be attained in HIV treatment. Perhaps the most sobering data comes from Paterson et al. (2000), who reported that virologic failure occurred in 72% of individuals with less than 95% adherence but in only 22% of individuals with 95% or greater adherence. More recent data (e.g., Bangsberg, 2006) reveals that these percentages vary depending on the type of medication regimen. However, the findings underscore the central importance of adherence for treatment success and demonstrate the need for near perfect levels of medication adherence to attain viral suppression. Thus less than optimal adherence in HIV illness has unparalleled consequences and unprecedented relevance to treatment success.

Targets of Treatment for CBT-AD

HAART is a difficult treatment regimen and requires a continued effort on the part of the patient to take his or her medication on time and to follow the proper food and liquid intake instructions at levels of near perfection. The Life-Steps module of this manual teaches a comprehensive set of skills necessary in order to avoid forgetting or missing medication doses. As in other chronic illnesses, there is now a large body of evidence that suggests that adherence to HAART is negatively affected by the presence of depression. Our research suggests that successful treatment of depression with CBT-AD in HIV-infected patients can improve the ability of patients to learn the Life-Steps strategies to improve adherence and maintain these improvements over time. The use of cognitive strategies to challenge negative beliefs about treatment and beliefs about HIV is a core element of our intervention. Activity scheduling, in addition to being an effective intervention for the treatment of depression, can also help patients to better plan for their HAART doses. Encouraging communication with the health care team is also essential, as patients taking HAART are likely to experience side effects of treatment and need to be proactive in finding ways to address them with their physician. Openness about side effects and addressing them will help patients to resist engaging in the common practice of skipping or altering doses in an attempt to avoid these side effects.

Diabetes (Diabetes Mellitus)

Diabetes mellitus is characterized by elevations in blood glucose resulting from defects in insulin secretion, insulin action, or both. Diabetes is a highly common illness, affecting over 150 million people worldwide, with prevalence rates increasing rapidly in many countries, including the United States. Much of this increase is concentrated in developed countries in which population aging, unhealthy diet, obesity, and sedentary lifestyle appear to be contributing to the rise.

There are four types of diabetes: type 1, type 2, gestational diabetes, and types that arise from genetic syndromes, drugs, and physical stressors such as surgery. This chapter discusses type 1 diabetes, which accounts for 5 to 10% of all cases of diabetes, and type 2 diabetes, which accounts for about 90% of all cases.

The treatment of diabetes, whether type 1 or 2, depends to a large extent on the patient's self-management. In contrast to HIV, in which there is predominately one major self-care behavior, medication adherence, diabetes requires many self-care behaviors, sometimes therefore referred to as "lifestyle management." This can include self-monitoring of blood glucose, adherence to diet and exercise recommendations, and regular attendance and active participation at medical appointments. For many patients it will also include adherence to medication and/or insulin self-administration.

Key Terms

- **Insulin:** This is a hormone produced by beta cells in the pancreas. Carbohydrates (or sugars) are absorbed from the intestines into the bloodstream after a meal. Insulin is then secreted by the pancreas in response to this detected increase in blood glucose (or sugar). Cells in the body can only absorb glucose when insulin is attached to their receptors. If a person has problems with insulin production or with sensitivity of cells to insulin, as in the case of diabetes, the cells cannot metabolize glucose to produce energy.

- **Blood glucose:** Carbohydrates are broken down into a simple sugar called glucose, which passes through the wall of the intestines into the bloodstream. All patients with diabetes should monitor their blood glucose levels in order to assess how well their diabetes is controlled. Good control means getting as close to a normal blood glucose level as possible. Ideally, this means levels between 90 and 130 mg/dl before meals and less than 180 mg/dl 2 hours after starting a meal.

- **Type 1 diabetes:** This type of diabetes was previously referred to as juvenile-onset or insulin-dependent diabetes and is caused by failure of pancreatic beta cells to produce insulin. These beta cells are actually destroyed by a process that may be related to a malfunction of the immune system. It can be diagnosed in children or adults. Patients with type 1 diabetes require daily injections of insulin.

- **Type 2 diabetes:** This type was previously called non-insulin-dependent or adult-onset diabetes. In type 2 diabetes, pancreatic beta cells still produce insulin, but not enough. Compounding the problems, the body's cells do not respond properly to the available insulin to adequately process glucose. This malfunction in the cells' receptivity to insulin is called insulin resistance. It is often associated with being overweight. Pancreatic beta cell function decreases over time, so that many patients eventually require treatment with oral medications and/or insulin.

- **HbA_{1c}:** The goal for patients with diabetes is to keep their HbA_{1c} below 7%. A blood test called Hemoglobin A1c or glycohemoglobin (or glycosylated hemoglobin) (HbA_{1c}) can be used to assess control of diabetes. Hemoglobin is a protein found inside red blood cells, which is responsible for transporting oxygen from the lungs to all the cells of the body. Excess glucose enters red blood cells and adheres, or glycates, to molecules of hemoglobin. The more excess glucose in the blood, the more hemoglobin gets glycated. It is possible to measure the percentage of glycosylated hemoglobin in the blood through a laboratory test. This test gives a picture of the average blood glucose control for the preceding 2 to 3 months and should be conducted routinely by a patient's provider. There is some variation in the meaning of levels of HbA_{1c} from one lab to another.

■ **Ketoacidosis**: A serious problem that can occur if blood glucose levels get so high that the body turns to its fat stores for energy, leading to the production of ketones, which can be found in the urine. This is more likely in people who have type 1 diabetes, but it can also occur, though much less frequently, in type 2 diabetes. Ketoacidosis is a significant cause of mortality in young persons with type 1 diabetes and often requires hospitalization for treatment. Poor adherence to insulin therapy is often the suspected cause.

Diabetes and Complications

Both type 1 and type 2 diabetes increase a patient's risk for many serious complications, including cardiovascular disease, retinopathy (noninflammatory damage to the retina of the eye), neuropathy (nerve damage), and nephropathy (kidney damage). For example, studies have shown that up to 60% of adults with diabetes also have high blood pressure and nearly all have one or more lipid abnormalities, such as increased triglycerides, low HDL cholesterol, or elevated LDL cholesterol. The American Diabetes Association reports that two out of three people with diabetes die from heart disease and stroke. Diabetes can also cause damage to the kidneys due to the increased filtering caused by high levels of blood sugar. This damage can be treated if detected early but could result in end-stage renal disease. Patients with diabetes are 40% more likely to suffer from glaucoma and 60% more likely to develop cataracts and are at risk to develop retinopathy, which can result in blindness. Thus it is important that patients with diabetes obtain regular eye exams to screen for early abnormalities. About half of all patients with diabetes have some form of nerve damage, or neuropathy. Peripheral diabetic neuropathy can lead to problems including pain, numbness, and weakness in the hands and feet. Autonomic neuropathy can lead to digestive problems, incontinence, sexual difficulties, dizziness, and other problems. Skin disorders and foot complications are also common, and foot ulcers are a particularly dangerous complication of diabetes, as they can lead to amputation. Diabetes patients face many potentially serious complications, and their risk for these complications depends to a large extent on how well their diabetes is controlled over time.

Importance of Adherence to Treatment Success

It is estimated that more than 95% of diabetes care consists of self-care behaviors (Anderson, 1995). Nonadherence can lead to worse glycemic control and worse blood pressure and lipid levels, which can result in increased rates of both microvascular complications, such as eye and kidney disease and nerve damage, and macrovascular complications, such as cardiovascular disease. Vascular and nerve damage combine to increase the risk of gangrene, which, in turn, can lead to amputation of lower limbs, reduced life expectancy, and overall poor quality of life (Rubin & Peyrot, 1999, 2001).

The Diabetes Control and Complications Trial was conducted from 1983 to 1993 by the National Institute of Diabetes and Digestive and Kidney Diseases (NIDDK) and had a profound influence on the care of diabetes worldwide. The study showed that keeping blood glucose levels as close to normal as possible, whether through lifestyle change or pharmacotherapy, slows the onset and progression of eye, kidney, and nerve diseases caused by type 1 diabetes. In fact, it demonstrated that any sustained lowering of blood glucose helps, even if the person has a history of poor control. Tight control reduced the risk of eye disease by 76%, kidney disease by 50%, and nerve disease by 60% (Diabetes Control and Complications Trial Research Group, 1993). Subsequent large trials among individuals with type 2 diabetes also showed that tighter glucose control could prevent the severe long-term complications of diabetes (Ohkubo et al., 1995; Reichard, Nilsson, & Rosenqvist, 1993; Turner, Cull, & Holman, 1996). Thus, perhaps to a greater extent than any other chronic illness, the burden of diabetes control falls on the shoulders of the patient and relies on his or her ability to adhere to lifestyle, medication, and glucose monitoring recommendations in order to achieve tight control.

Self-monitoring of blood glucose is recommended as the core element of self-management in diabetes (e.g., Holmes & Griffiths, 2002). Self-monitoring of blood glucose is intended to allow the patient to collect information on blood glucose levels at different time points and identify high blood glucose levels in a timely manner (Nathan, 1996; Karter, 2001). We target self-monitoring of blood glucose as a core self-care behavior in our diabetes program because knowledge of glucose levels allows patients to engage in other health-related self-care behaviors, such as adjusting insulin dosages, diet, or medications and seeking medical care in response.

Medication adherence is another important aspect of self-care in diabetes. Most patients require multiple medications, possibly including exogenous insulin, to control hyperglycemia. Most patients will also be taking medications to control the associated metabolic risk factors of hypertension and hyperlipidemia. Investigators have argued that improved treatment adherence to these regimens can close the gap between the potential efficacy of these treatments and the benefits patients actually receive from treatment (e.g., Rubin, 2005; Piette, Heisler, & Wagner, 2004; Schectman, Nadkarni, & Voss, 2002).

Diet, exercise, and other self-care behaviors are also important for both type 1 and type 2 diabetes patients. Patients with type 1 diabetes must carefully balance food intake, insulin, and physical activity. Patients with type 2 diabetes are often prescribed oral medications that increase insulin production, decrease insulin resistance, or block carbohydrate absorption. They may also require the administration of exogenous insulin. Because these treatments improve metabolic control, they may result in weight gain if patients do not reduce their food intake and increase physical activity. For type 2 diabetes, weight loss is often an important treatment goal, as reducing weight improves insulin resistance and reduces risk of cardiovascular complic

diet are central health behaviors in the self-mar

ditional self-care behaviors such as proper foot

cers are important and can be especially impor

ropathy. Smoking cessation is also an import

are current smokers, as smoking reduces bloc

including feet, that may already be comprom__

complications of diabetes and consistent attendance at medical visits are important for all patients.

Targets of Treatment for CBT-AD

Diabetes self-management is complex and demanding. It is also a long-term endeavor, as there is no cure currently available for diabetes. As patients age, they may deal with increasing numbers of complications, as well as other comorbid illnesses that also require management. The second module in this manual, called Life-Steps, includes a comprehensive set of skills that can be applied to the self-management of diabetes. As in other chronic illnesses, there is now a large body of evidence that suggests that adherence to diabetes self-care is negatively affected by the presence of depression (e.g., Gonzalez et al., in press). Our research suggests that successful treatment of depression with CBT-AD in diabetes patients can improve their ability to learn the Life-Steps strategies to improve adherence and maintain these improvements over time. The use of cognitive strategies to challenge negative beliefs about treatment and about diabetes is a core element of our intervention. Activity scheduling, in addition to being an effective intervention for the treatment of depression, can also help patients better plan self-monitoring of their blood glucose, medications, and insulin doses. Activity scheduling can also focus on establishing regular exercise routines and planning regular healthy meals. Encouraging communication with the health care team is also essential. Patients are potentially the best source of information about their diabetes if they have been monitoring blood glucose and their self-care activities. This information can have important influences on treatment alterations, such as increasing medication doses, changing medications that may not be effective for a given patient, or adding exogenous insulin to the treatment regimen.

In the preceding sections we provided information about HIV and diabetes, as these are the two conditions for which this intervention was specifically developed. However, many other chronic medical conditions require a high level of patient self-management in order to control the illness. This self-management can involve adhering to medications, attending medical visits, making changes in diet, losing weight, increasing physical activity, and self-monitoring of symptoms. In the following sections we briefly review chronic illnesses for which the CBT-AD intervention may be especially applicable. However, in addition to the illnesses, there are other conditions for which CBT-AD may be useful. For example, self-management demands can be high in patients being considered for, or who have recently undergone, organ transplant, or who are being treated for tuberculosis, epilepsy, or end-stage renal disease. Depression may also be a concern for many patients undergoing such treatments. As depression is more common in patients with chronic illness than in the general population, and because self-management is an integral component of the treatment of most chronic illnesses, it is likely that the CBT-AD intervention will have far-reaching applications. As a guide for clinicians, we review information about hypertension, coronary heart disease, asthma, and hepatitis C and about cancer patients taking oral chemotherapy. These may be some of the most frequent diseases that involve self-care/adherence, which can be affected by depression.

Hypertension

Hypertension, or high blood pressure, is usually defined as having a systolic blood pressure of 140 mm Hg or greater, having diastolic blood pressure of 90 mm Hg or greater, or taking antihypertensive medications. Hypertension is a global problem and has been identified as the leading risk factor for mortality (Ezzati, Lopez, Rogers, Vander Hoorn, & Murray, 2002). Recent estimates suggest that more than a quarter of the world's adult population, totaling nearly 1 billion people, had hypertension in 2000. This proportion is expected to increase to 29%—1.56 billion people—by 2025 (Kearney, Whelton, Reynolds, Muntner, & Whelton, 2005). In the United States, at least 65 million adults had hypertension in 1999–2000, with a total hypertension prevalence rate of 31.3% (Fields et al., 2004). Hypertension places patients at increased risk of stroke, myocardial infarction, congestive heart failure, kidney failure, and peripheral vascular disease. For example, hypertension increases the risk of ischemic heart disease three- to fourfold and of overall cardiovascular risk by two- to threefold (Berenson et al., 1998).

Treatment and the accompanying adherence behaviors required for hypertension depend on the severity of the elevation in blood pressure and the presence of other comorbid conditions such as diabetes. For less severe hypertension, lifestyle changes are emphasized, including losing weight, increasing activity, and eating a balanced diet. For more severe hypertension, prescribed medications are used in conjunction with lifestyle changes. Although pharmacotherapy to reduce hypertension has been proven to be effective, adequate control remains challenging, with only one-quarter of patients achieving adequate control. This low level of treatment success is thought to be largely a result of medication nonadherence. Good adherence to medication has been associated with improved blood pressure control and reduced complications of hypertension.

In addition to adherence to medications, lifestyle factors are also important in the management of hypertension. Increasing physical activity and/or aerobic exercise, losing weight, restricting sodium intake, and moderating alcohol intake may all be important self-management goals for patients with hypertension. Data from the National Health and Nutrition Examination Survey suggest that depression predicts the onset of hypertension and thus would be more prevalent in patients with hypertension (Jonas, Franks, & Ingram, 1997). There is also evidence that depressive symptoms are associated with nonadherence to antihypertensive treatment (Wang et al., 2002). Therefore, it is likely that patients with hypertension who also present with problems with depression could benefit from CBT-AD.

Coronary Heart Disease

Coronary heart disease (CHD) is the leading cause of death in the United States, causing one of every five deaths in the United States in 2004. Recent estimates suggest that an estimated 15,800,000 American adults suffer from CHD. Of these, approximately 7,900,000 have had myocardial infarction (MI; i.e., a heart attack), and 8,900,000 suffer from angina pectoris (i.e., chest pain). The estimated annual incidence of MI is 565,000 new attacks and 300,000 recurrent attacks annually. A conservative estimate for the number of hospital discharges with acute coronary syndrome, defined as either acute MI or acute unstable angina, in 2004 is 840,000. The estimated direct and indirect cost of CHD for 2007 is $151.6 billion (American Heart Association, 2007). Thus CHD is a very common disorder and results in significant morbidity, mortality, and cost. Depression and nonadherence are two related psychosocial factors that have been extensively researched in CHD and are each associated with poorer health outcomes.

Physically healthy individuals with depression are 1.5 to 2 times more likely to have an onset of CHD than those without depression. Among those with existing CHD, those with depression are 1.5 to 2 times more likely to suffer from cardiac morbidity and mortality than those who do not have depression (Lett et al., 2004). Post-myocardial infarction patients with a clinician-diagnosed depressive disorder or self-reported depressive symptoms are between 2 and 2.5 times more likely to have a new cardiovascular event and/or to die from a cardiovascular event than those who are not diagnosed with depression (Van Melle et al., 2004). Major depression has been reported in 15–20% of patients hospitalized for acute MI, and approximately 45% have been found to have either major or minor depression (Schleifer et al., 1989; Frasure-Smith, Lesperance, & Talajic, 1993; Frasure-Smith, Lesperance, & Talajic, 1995a; Ladwig, Kieser, Konig, Breithardt, & Borggrefe, 1991).

Data from post-MI patients suggests that depression negatively impacts self-care and adherence following discharge. Patients who had had an acute MI in the previous 3–5 days and who had symptoms of mild to moderate depression, major depression, and/or dysthymia had lower adherence to a low-fat diet, regular exercise, stress reduction, and increasing social support at 4 months follow-up. Those with major depression and/or dysthymia also reported taking medications as prescribed less often than those without major depression and/or dysthymia (Ziegelstein et al., 2000). A recent study that followed patients after hospitalization for acute MI or unstable angina found that depression predicted nonadherence to aspirin in a gradient fashion, with higher levels of depressive symptoms predicting more nonadherence. Furthermore, improvements in depressive symptoms in the first month after discharge were associated with improvements in adherence rates in the subsequent 2 months (Rieckmann et al., 2006).

Nonadherence to recommended lifestyle changes (increasing physical activity, weight loss, dietary changes) and medication regimens has been associated with decreased survival for CHD patients in a number of studies (e.g., Horwitz et al., 1990; McDermott, Schmitt, & Wallner, 1997). Therefore, it is possible that the relationship between depression and worse health outcomes in CHD patients could be at least partly explained by associated medical nonadherence. Thus the research evidence is supportive for the efficacy of CBT-AD, which could improve both depression and medical adherence in patients with CHD.

Asthma

Asthma is a chronic disease that involves inflammation of the airways superimposed with recurrent episodes of limited airflow, mucus production, and cough. Asthma is generally diagnosed by periodic experiences of symptoms of wheezing, nocturnal awakening from asthma, cough, difficulty breathing, chest tightness, and episodic decreases and variability in pulmonary function. Asthma is a common and costly public health problem affecting 17 million Americans at an annual cost of $11 billion (Mannino, Homa, Akinbami, Ford, & Redd, 2002; Weiss & Sullivan, 2001). Although effective treatments which have been shown to dramatically reduce morbidity are available, nonadherence to these treatments is a widespread problem among patients.

Treatment of asthma and accompanying adherence behaviors involve avoiding triggers, self-monitoring of symptoms and lung functioning, and taking two types of medications aimed at the two components of asthma: airway inflammation and acute bronchoconstriction. Corticosteroids are a commonly used anti-inflammatory medication for people suffering from asthma. These and other anti-inflammatory drugs reduce swelling and mucus production in the airways and are usually prescribed for daily intake. Anti-inflammatory medications control inflammation and prevent chronic symptoms such as coughing or breathlessness at night, in the early morning, or after exertion. Quick-relief medications are also used to address asthma attack symptoms (cough, chest tightness, and wheezing) when attacks occur. Avoiding asthma triggers such as inhaled allergens and certain foods and medications, irritants such as tobacco smoke, and other triggers is also important. Lastly, self-monitoring of daily asthma symptoms and peak airflow with a flow meter and recording information in a diary is another important aspect of self-management.

Nonadherence to daily inhaled corticosteroid therapy is probably the most important barrier to achieving optimal asthma control. Major deficits in other self-management behaviors, such as peak flow meter use, inhaler technique, titration of medications, trigger avoidance, proper response to symptoms, and flow meter readings, have also been documented. The chronic nature of asthma and the need for long-term and consistent treatment is often not clearly understood by patients. Researchers have noted that conceptualizing asthma as an acute, episodic illness may have an internal logic of its own based on the experience of the disease by patients. The experience of attacks with little apparent warning may encourage patients to think of asthma as a series of unexpected, acute episodes separated by "disease-free" periods. The focus on attacks and relief experienced when a severe episode is terminated may encourage patients to discount the importance of low-level symptoms and breathing impairment that persist in between attacks. In fact, patients may think, "no symptoms, no asthma," and this type of episodic belief was found to be associated with inaccurate understanding of asthma and with one-third lower odds of adherence to inhaled corticosteroids when asymptomatic (Halm, Mora, & Leventhal, 2006).

Patients with asthma appear particularly likely to suffer from psychological problems, especially anxiety disorders. Studies have reported associations between depressive disorders and anxiety disorders and worse asthma control and quality of life, with one recent study showing that although both depressive disorders and anxiety disorders are associated with worse asthma-related quality of life, only depressive disorders are associated with worse asthma control (Lavoie et al., 2006). Among inner-city asthma patients recently discharged from hospitalization, symptoms of depression were found to be quite common, and high levels of depressive symptoms were shown to predict worse adherence to therapy after discharge (Smith et al., 2006). Thus there is evidence to suggest that CBT-AD, with a particular focus on correcting misperceptions about the chronicity of asthma and the need for continued treatment and self-monitoring, could be effective for asthma patients with depression.

Hepatitis C

The hepatitis C virus (HCV) is a major public health problem and is the leading cause of death from chronic liver disease in the United States (Kim, 2002). In the United States, more than 2.7 million people are estimated to have ongoing HCV infection (Alter et al., 1999), and the most recent World Health Organization estimate of the prevalence of HCV infection is 2%, representing 123 million people worldwide (Perz, Farrington, & Pecoraro, 2004). The most common risk factors for HCV infection include blood transfusion before 1992, when sensitive screening became available in the United States; intravenous drug use; and unsafe sex. In the United States, injection drug use is the primary risk factor.

Among patients with chronic HCV infection, 5–20% are reported to develop cirrhosis over periods of approximately 20–25 years. Persons with HCV-related cirrhosis are at risk for developing end-stage liver disease, as well as carcinoma of the liver. Between 15 and 45% of persons with acute HCV will recover, are not at risk of long-term complications, and do not need treatment. However, patients with chronic HCV face a life-threatening illness. The progression to cirrhosis of the liver is the primary concern, although the rate of progression is usually slow. It often takes more than two decades and occurs more often in persons infected at older ages, particularly men; those who drink more than 50 grams of alcohol each day; those who are obese or have substantial hepatic steatosis (accumulation of fat in liver cells); or those with HIV coinfection (Strader, Wright, Thomas, & Seef, 2004).

The efficacy of available treatments has increased consistently since HCV was identified in 1989. The goal of treatment is to eradicate the virus to avoid these long-term complications of chronic HCV. The most effective current combination treatment available consists of weekly subcutaneous injections of long-acting peginterferon alfa and oral ribavirin, usually taken over a period of at least 48 weeks. This currently represents the standard of care in the United States. Rates of sustained virological response vary depending on the genotype of HCV and the severity of the infection (as measured by viral load). However, approximately 46 to 77% of patients achieve a successful response after 48 weeks of maximal dose combination therapy (Strader, Wright, Thomas, & Seef, 2004).

Although effective, combination therapy commonly causes side effects, including fatigue, influenza-like symptoms, gastrointestinal disturbances, neuropsychiatric symptoms (especially depression), and hematologic abnormalities. Approximately 75% of treated patients experience one or more side effect of combination therapy that may require dose reduction or drug discontinuation, and many patients with HCV discontinue or are nonadherent to treatment because of these side effects.

Patients with HCV appear to have higher rates of psychiatric illness, especially substance abuse/dependence and depression. Rates of depression in patients with HCV have been reported to range from 22 to 49% (e.g., Kraus, Schafer, Csef, Scheurlen, & Faller, 2000; El-Serag, Kunik, Richardson, & Rabeneck, 2002). Of major concern, estimates suggest that between 23 and 40% of patients treated for HCV will develop major depression during therapy (e.g., Dieperink, Ho, Thuras, & Willenbring, 2003; Bonaccorso et al., 2002) and that combination therapy can biomedically induce depression.

There is growing evidence that antidepressants can be useful in the treatment of interferon-induced depression (e.g., Hauser et al., 2002; Gleason, Yates, Isbell, & Phillipsen, 2002). There is also preliminary evidence that integrating mental health care (including providing cognitive-behavioral therapy) with medical care in the treatment of chronic HCV can improve treatment adherence (Knott et al., 2006). Although randomized trials of cognitive-behavioral therapy are currently lacking, the evidence from the research literature that is available suggests that approaches such as CBT-AD, which integrate CBT for depression directly with adherence skills training, could have an important application in the treatment of depression and the improvement of treatment adherence in patients undergoing treatment for HCV.

The availability of oral chemotherapies promises to have a significant impact on the treatment of various forms of cancer in the future. Several oral chemotherapy agents have already become available, and many more are being evaluated in efficacy research trials. Currently, only 5% of cancer chemotherapy agents are available in oral formulation; however, oral agents represent an estimated 20–25% of all drugs in development (Bedell, Hartigan, Wilkinson, & Halpern, 2002; Birner, 2003). Oral chemotherapy agents have applications across a variety of cancers, including multiple myeloma (bone marrow), breast, liver, lung, and colorectal cancer. Although these oral formulations offer significant advantages over standard intravenous treatments, including greater convenience and shorter treatment time, they also require patients to self-monitor for side effects, and they rely on adherence to prescribed regimens in order to achieve their effects. There is also a resultant decrease in contact with health care providers as treatment can be self-administered. Although cancer patients may be thought to be highly motivated to adhere to therapy because of the gravity of their disease (Waterhouse, Calzone, Mele, & Brenner, 1993), nonadherence rates of 43–50%, respectively, have been reported in samples of breast cancer and hematologic malignancy patients taking oral agents (Lebovits et al., 1990).

There are various reasons for nonadherence to these new treatments, including the common occurrence of nausea, either resulting from the cancer or as a side effect of treatment. Nausea may make it difficult for patients to take and retain oral chemotherapy agents. Adherence to strict administration schedules may also be challenging for some patients. There is also the possibility that patients may adjust doses without consulting their health care providers for various reasons, including worrying that oral treatments are not effective enough, to avoid side effects, and to reduce the cost of oral agents, which are often not covered by insurance plans (Bedell, 2003).

As the American Cancer Society (2006) has estimated that more than 25% of patients with cancer undergoing treatment become clinically depressed, it is likely that many patients on oral chemotherapy will experience depression that could interfere with their adherence to these therapies. Depressed individuals have been found to be less likely to adhere to their oncologists' treatment recommendations (e.g., Goodwin, Zhang, & Ostir, 2004), and, as patients assume more of the responsibility for correctly administering oral chemotherapy, it is likely that depression would be associated with nonadherence. Therefore, it is likely that depressed cancer patients taking oral chemotherapy could benefit from CBT-AD.

Summary

In general, depression is a common condition that co-occurs with medical illness. Depression in and of itself is a distressing and interfering condition. In addition, the primary and associated symptoms of depression can dramatically affect the self-care behaviors needed to maintain a medical treatment regimen. Regardless of the specific adherence behavior required, the approach of integrating CBT, the most widely studied psychosocial treatment for depression, with adherence-promoting behaviors can have significant impacts on the health of clients who are managing a chronic illness. This intervention is described in the forthcoming chapters.

Chapter 3

Module 1: Psychoeducation About CBT and Motivational Interviewing

(Corresponds to chapters 1 and 2 of the workbook)

Materials Needed

- CBT model of depression

- Motivational Exercise: Pros and Cons of Changing

Outline

- Set agenda

- Review depression score on CES-D and discuss with client

- Review client's treatment adherence over the previous week

- Discuss any relationship between depression and adherence

- Provide information about how depression can negatively affect medical adherence

- Discuss client's symptoms and create a CBT model of depression for the client

- Review motivational information and exercise

- Discuss the structure of the sessions

Set Agenda

Begin every session by interactively setting an agenda with the client. This helps maintain a structured focus and allows you and the client to agree on the most important topics for problem solving. In this module, the session focus is on exploring the relationship between depression and adherence.

Review of Depression Severity on CES-D

As will be done at the beginning of every session, the client completes the CES-D self-report measure of depression, which can be found in the corresponding workbook. Briefly review his or her score and take note of any symptoms that may have changed from the last measurement, if one was done previously (e.g., at an intake session). As therapy progresses, it can be helpful to review the total score for each of the preceding sessions in order to examine what might be helpful in treatment and what might not. This may also be a discussion point regarding future therapy "homework" and tracking what interventions result in measurable progress—that is, if a client completes the "homework" and feels better, this can be emphasized. If the client has not engaged in behavioral change and his or her symptoms of depression have not changed, this could be utilized to increase motivation in future sessions. This can be facilitated by adding the CES-D score in the client's medical or mental health record so that it is easy to review and track over time.

You may also track the client's progress through the use of the Progress Summary Chart, which charts improvement session by session. The version for therapists includes session-by-session CES-D scores, adherence scores, homework assignments for the following week, a homework rating for the previous week, and a place to record the particular module covered. This chart can also be used to examine whether the client is getting worse in terms of depression and therefore whether additional treatment is needed (i.e., referral for medications, medication augmentation, or hospitalization). The version for clients in the workbook tracks similar information so that clients can actively see their progress.

A blank copy of the Progress Summary Tracking Chart, as well as a completed example (figure 3.4), is provided at the end of this chapter. Because you will use this chart for more than one client with this approach, you may photocopy it from the book or download multiple copies from the Treatments *ThatWork*™ website at http://www.oup.com/us/ttw.

A CES-D score of 16 is typically used as a cutoff to screen in for clinical depression. It is important to assess suicidality in each session, particularly if CES-D scores are high or if they have increased by more than 25% from the previous session. In this way, an appropriate further intervention or referral for a more intensive intervention (i.e., medications if the client is not already prescribed medications, or hospital-level care) can be employed to prevent exacerbation of depression or suicidality.

Review of Adherence and Any Medical Changes

The client also completes the Weekly Adherence Assessment Form. This form is included in the corresponding client workbook. Although treatment has just started, the client should complete this form in order to establish a baseline against which his or her improvement in adherence behaviors throughout treatment can be measured. Have the client use the form to assess any medical changes experienced over the preceding week, including changes in symptoms or emergence of new symptoms, or new test results (e.g., viral load for HIV-infected clients or blood glucose testing for clients with diabetes). Also discuss the relation of these medical changes to adherence behavior and correlation with mood. Positive medical changes can be used to reinforce improvements in adherence behaviors. Conversely, providing feedback to clients regarding the exacerbation of their symptoms or test results may be a good opportunity to address barriers to and increase motivation for medical adherence. It may also allow for renegotiating the planned medical regimen to better adapt to client needs.

A sample, filled-out Weekly Adherence Assessment Form is shown in figure 3.1.

Depression and Adherence

The purpose of this first module is to teach the client about depression in the context of having chronic illness. The emphasis is on how each of the components of depression (cognitive, behavioral, physical) adds to a cycle of continued or worsening of symptoms and decreases abilities

Weekly Adherence Assessment Form

Note: This form is to be completed by the client at the start of every session. Adherence goals should be determined during the adherence counseling (Life-Steps) module and should correspond to the articulated adherence goals. Examples are shown in script.

Thinking about the **PAST WEEK**, on average how would you rate your ability to adhere to your goal of _taking all of my medications_____?

(Check one)

Very poor	Poor	Fair	Good	Very good	Excellent
☐	☐	☐	☐	☐	☐

Thinking about the **PAST WEEK**, on average how would you rate your ability to adhere to your goal of _monitoring my blood glucose once a day_____?

(Check one)

Very poor	Poor	Fair	Good	Very good	Excellent
☐	☐	☐	☐	☐	☐

Thinking about the **PAST WEEK**, on average how would you rate your ability to adhere to your goal of _exercising three times a week_____?

(Check one)

Very poor	Poor	Fair	Good	Very good	Excellent
☐	☐	☐	☐	☐	☐

Thinking about the **PAST WEEK**, on average how would you rate your ability to adhere to your goal of _avoiding high-fat foods_____?

(Check one)

Very poor	Poor	Fair	Good	Very good	Excellent
☐	☐	☐	☐	☐	☐

Figure 3.1

Example of Completed Weekly Adherence Assessment Form

to adhere to one's medical regimen. This module is meant to lay the groundwork for the remainder of the treatment.

Credibility and confidence in a treatment is critical for the treatment to be successful. Hence, this module is of particular importance, because clients need to understand the rationale behind CBT-AD in order for them to have the motivation to engage in the treatment. Of particular importance is making the model relevant to the particular client's needs. This can take some therapist skill and requires eliciting information about the client's current difficulties with adherence and depression and incorporating them into the discussion of the model. **We have found that the best way to present this is through a highly interactive discussion rather than a didactic presentation.**

Components of Depression

Your discussion of depression can be brief, as the main explanation of the three components should come from the interactive discussion of the client's symptoms.

Cognitive Component

The cognitive component of depression consists of negative thoughts that people have when they are depressed. This can be exacerbated by stressors associated with chronic illness and may include negative thoughts about treatment.

Behavioral Component

The behavioral component of depression refers to the particular behaviors that a person does or avoids when depressed. It is important to note that these very behaviors can lead to further increases in depression. Avoidance of activities that normally would result in enjoyment is a key issue. Additionally, individuals with depression also have difficulty with normal problem solving due to decreased motivation and negative thinking. This can certainly affect adherence and self-care behaviors.

Physiological Component

Physical symptoms of depression include low energy, decreased appetite, fatigue, sleep problems, and concentration problems. These symptoms can be exacerbated by chronic illness and/or medications, and therefore they also affect adherence. In HIV, for example, fatigue can be a prominent symptom that can lead to increased depression. In diabetes, insulin variability and glycemic status can be associated with mood variations.

CBT Model of Depression

Complete the cognitive-behavioral model of depression shown in figure 3.2 with your client and fill in specific symptoms in each category. Development of the CBT model should be an interactive process. Write the specific cognitions, behaviors, and physiological symptoms that the client reports experiencing when depressed.

Having the client understand the CBT model and how it specifically applies to him or her is, in many ways, the basis for the entire remainder of this intervention package. This discussion typically comprises a significant portion of the session and ensures that the client understands the model and how it explains the maintenance of depressed mood and consequently affects his or her self-care. It is imperative that the client totally understand this model. You must use language that is understandable to the client. For example, the word *cognitive,* although it is the name of the treatment (i.e. "cognitive-behavioral therapy"), may be difficult for some clients to understand in this context. Instead, words such as *thoughts* and *beliefs* may help the client see the association of cognitions and emotions.

Given the high importance of these concepts, we recommend that you make sure to take sufficient time with this model. In fact, sometimes this may take an entire session (or two) for some clients. Completing the form interactively with them and having the clients take notes in their workbooks (or you can take notes and provide a handout) can be a useful adjunct to this session, so that you and the client can continue to refer back to this as the treatment progresses.

Complete interactively with participant, filling in specific symptoms in each category.

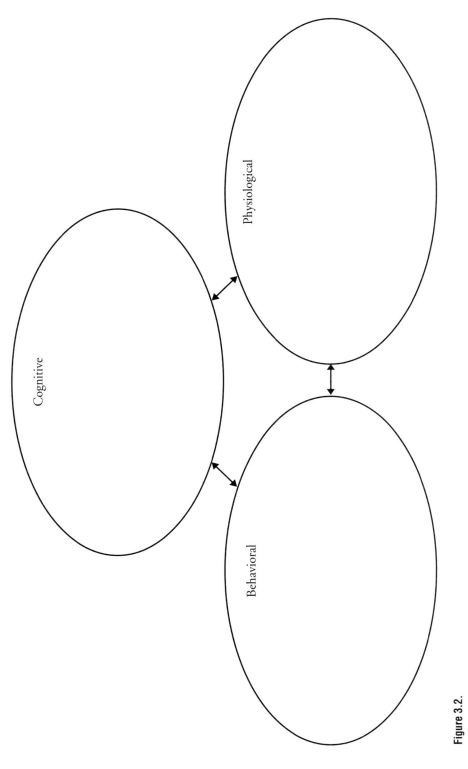

Figure 3.2.

Cognitive-Behavioral Model of Depression

Probe questions about each dimension:

- Behavioral: *What types of things do you think you avoid, or do less often, because you are depressed? What kinds of things do you do more of because you are depressed?*

- Cognitive: *What is your thinking like since you have become depressed? What thoughts do you have about yourself? Your relationships with others? Your future? Your illness? Your treatment/medications? Think of the last time you were really feeling down. Picture where you were. What was going through your mind at that time?*

- Physiological: *What physical symptoms do you experience? Do you have trouble sleeping? Trouble concentrating? Appetite changes? Fatigue or low energy?*

- Role of chronic illness: *How does having your illness contribute to your thoughts, your behaviors, and your physical symptoms?*

- Adhering to medical regimen: *What happens to the way you take care of yourself when you are feeling depressed? What is the result? How does this end up affecting your mood?*

Cycle of Depression

Use the following sample dialogue to show how the client's reported symptoms function together to form a cycle of depression.

A person who has these kinds of thoughts going through his or her head is less likely to do these activities and is more likely to withdraw from others. Not doing these activities and being isolated are going to make you more likely to feel like you have less energy and more fatigue. These changes are going to make you feel more depressed and are going to make you more likely to have these kinds of negative thoughts. This cycle just builds on itself in a downward spiral toward depression, unless we do something to break these connections.

Focus of Treatment

Explain to the client that the point of this treatment is to attack each of the three components of depression and to break the connection between them. Provide a brief overview of each of the modules that compose this treatment program, how they address each component of depression, and how they will be used to help medical adherence.

1. Life-Steps will teach skills that facilitate medical adherence and decrease the negative impact of depression on adherence behavior.

2. Activity scheduling will address the behavioral component of depression by increasing mood-improving activities and decreasing or eliminating behaviors that contribute to depression (e.g., avoidance and withdrawal).

3. Cognitive restructuring will teach clients to challenge negative thoughts that contribute to depression and develop more adaptive ways of thinking.

4. Problem solving will help clients develop better coping strategies to deal with problems that can contribute to depression.

5. Relaxation training will give clients tools to address the physical symptoms of depression.

6. The module addressing maintenance of changes will help clients transition to "being their own therapist"—continuing the skills learned even in the context of emergent life stressors.

Therapist Note: If you are breaking this module into two sessions, this would be a natural stopping point. In this case, the next session should begin with a brief review as per the format of every session (set agenda, CES-D mood check, adherence check), followed by the next set of material.

Motivation for Alleviating Depression

Motivational interviewing (MI; Miller & Rollnick, 1991) interventions can help clients examine the impact of depression on their lives, including self-care, adherence, and functional impairment. The particular relevance of self-care when living with chronic illness is emphasized.

Discuss with your client his or her goals for participating in this program. What is his or her general motivation? Review the problem areas identified by the client in the initial evaluation and assessment. Talk about anticipated difficulties with following this program (e.g., attendance).

Relate the CBT model of depression to the client's problems. Ask: How does this model fit in with the difficulties you are having? How are these symptoms affected by your illness? Attempt to show how each section ties in with specific problems the client presents with.

Motivational Metaphor

Use the following metaphor to illustrate the cycle of depression:

As we discussed, depression is a cycle.

Because of being depressed, it's more difficult to motivate yourself to change, and because you haven't motivated yourself to change, you feel more depressed.

One way to think of this is an analogy of being stuck in a hole. Let's say that a person is stuck in a hole but that the only tool he or she has is a shovel. The person knows how to shovel, and it's an easy, comfortable thing to do. However, if the person does this—shovels—it makes the problem worse; the hole gets deeper.

One day, someone comes along and throws down a ladder. But the only thing the person knows how to do is shovel. Shoveling feels comfortable, but now there is another choice.

Not only that—there is a problem with the ladder. The ladder is scalding hot. So, climbing up will be painful and difficult, and shoveling will be comfortable and easy. However, choosing the ladder will get the person out of the hole. (Adapted from Linehan, 1993)

Work with the client to complete the Motivational Exercise: Pros and Cons of Changing, found in the workbook. Emphasize the negative effect of depression on the client's life. Questions should address topics regarding the client's hopes for living (e.g., goals not met, having children, enjoyable aspects of life, etc.). Be sure to go over each cell in the matrix on the worksheet and point out that there are pros and cons of changing and pros and cons of not changing. For example, a big "pro" of not changing is that one does not have to do the work to change. This may be different from a "con" of changing, which for some people may elicit different concerns, such as, "at least with my current situation, I know what things are like, and I am comfortable."

A sample completed Motivational Exercise form is shown in figure 3.3.

After completing this exercise on the pros and cons of changing, ask the client to rate his or her motivation to change his or her depression and to work on adherence to his or her medical regimen on a scale of 1–10, with 1 representing no motivation at all and 10 representing high motivation.

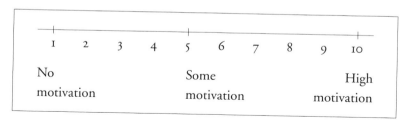

If the client gives a number other than 10, ask, "Why did you rate your motivation a _____ and not a 10?" This usually will facilitate a conversation about the client's reasons for wanting to be adherent; for example, "I really want to stay healthy," "I want to live a long life," and so forth. This is a good way to start the conversation. Then ask why the client did not give a higher number. This usually yields reasons for barriers. Use this as a discussion point to clarify the pros and cons of changing or what the treatment may be like. If the client appears to not be motivated at all to participate in this program, it may be necessary to progress through the treatment more slowly, trying to get the client to agree to try some portions of it and revisiting progress, and/or to con-

Motivational Exercise: Pros and Cons of Changing

	Pros	Cons
Changing: Working to improve depression	I will feel better and I will be able to take better care of myself. Maybe my illness will improve, or at least my condition won't deteriorate. I'll be able to be there for my family and spend more time with my children.	If I change, I won't know what to expect. At least I'm comfortable now. It may be hard work to make changes.
Not changing: Keeping things the way they are	I won't have to work hard and put a lot of effort into making a change.	If I don't change, my illness may worsen. I may not be able to work or accomplish other important goals.

Figure 3.3.

Example of Completed Motivational Exercise

sider alternate approaches. Finally, for some clients, giving a low number could mean that they do not fully understand the rationale behind the treatment nor have confidence that it applies to them. In this case, it may be useful to return to the cognitive-behavioral model to be sure that it is suited to the particular needs of your client.

Format of the Treatment

Explain to the client that the following activities are included in each session.

Setting an Agenda

It is important to begin each session by setting an agenda. This helps maintain a structured focus of the treatment on depression and medical adherence and also prepares the client for what lies ahead in the upcoming session.

You should be aware that one of the challenges in conducting psychological treatment in general, but particularly with clients with a medical illness and depression, is to avoid getting distracted by lengthy discussions of problems clients may be facing that are not focused on the present or on problem solving or skills training. At times, these discussions are pertinent to their depression and problems with adherence and can be integrated into the context of the session topics. Other times, it is necessary to convey empathy regarding a client's difficulty and acknowledge that one of the limitations of this treatment is the need to remain focused so that you both can go over all of the skills to manage depression and adherence. The general approach involves working with the client to take the emergent problems and apply them directly to the specific treatment modules.

Monitoring Progress

As we have already discussed, this treatment approach involves regularly monitoring improvement. By administering a measure of depression symptoms and reviewing medical adherence each week, you can determine whether the skills being taught are helping the client. Items that do not change on the depression assessment or patterns of difficulties with adherence can be targets for further discussion. We recommend using the CES-D. We find it important to start each session with a discussion of the current symptom score, as well as a review of the homework.

Reviewing Homework

At the end of each module (except this first one), you and the client work on a homework assignment. The homework is geared toward specifically practicing the new skills discussed during the session. The homework is then reviewed at the beginning of the following session.

It is important to acknowledge the client's incremental success and to problem-solve any barriers or difficulties he or she may be facing. Repetition and practice of new skills is critical for individuals with chronic illness to maximize gains made in treatment and to increase the likelihood of sustaining improvement. We provide a copy of the checklist for monitoring homework assignments at the end of this chapter, as well as in the workbook for the client.

Assigning Homework

As previously stated, at the end of each session you work with the client to assign homework exercises based on skills taught during treatment.

Addressing Concerns About Treatment

Before progressing to the next module, it is important to discuss with the client any concerns he or she may have about the treatment. If the client has had past experiences with therapy for depression, be sure to talk about this. Some questions to ask are, "What did you like or dislike about the last time you were in therapy for depression?" "Why did you decide to participate in this particular program?" "What was helpful, and what was particularly unhelpful?"

Progress Summary Chart

Date	Module Covered	CES-D Score	Adherence Rating	Homework Assigned	Past Week's Homework Rating

Progress Summary Chart

Date	Module Covered	CES-D Score	Adherence Rating	Homework Assigned	Past Week's Homework Rating
3/6	Psychoeducation and Motivational Interviewing	28	50%	N/A	N/A
3/13	Life-Steps	30	65%	Implement Adherence Action Items	2
3/20	Activity Scheduling	20	75%	-Practice Adherence -Complete Activity Log	3
3/27	Cognitive Restructuring I	18	60%	-Practice Adherence and Activity Scheduling -Complete first 4 columns of thought record	4
4/1	Cognitive Restructuring II	16	65%	-Practice Adherence and Activity Scheduling -Complete full thought record	3
4/8	Cognitive Restructuring II (cont'd)	12	85%	-Practice Adherence and Activity Scheduling -Practice Cognitive Restructuring and Rational Response	5
4/15	Problem Solving	10	100%	-Practice Adherence, Activity Scheduling, and Cognitive Restructuring -Complete Problem-Solving Sheet	5
4/22	Relaxation Training	8	100%	-Practice Adherence, Activity Scheduling, Cognitive Restructuring, and Problem Solving -Complete Relaxation Practice Log	4
4/29	Review, Maintenance, and Relapse Prevention	8	100%	-Continue to Practice Adherence, Activity Scheduling, Cognitive Restructuring, Problem Solving, and Relaxation -Practice Relapse Prevention -Complete 1-Month Review Sheet	5

Figure 3.4

Example of Completed Progress Summary Chart

Homework Rating Chart

Instructions: Please rate your practice of the following skills for depression treatment since your last session. Place a check in the column if you tried this skill. Only mark skills that you and your therapist discussed, because your therapist may go through modules in a different order from how they're presented in this manual. Also, it is useful to jot down some notes about your practice so that you can discuss this with your therapist. This can be done in the right-hand column.

Skills	✓	Notes About Your Homework Practice
Activity Scheduling Monitor activities and mood on a daily basis using Activity Log Incorporate activities that involve pleasure or mastery into daily schedule		
Cognitive Restructuring (Adaptive Thinking) Identify automatic thoughts Identify cognitive distortions Record automatic thoughts and match to distortions using Thought Record Challenge automatic thoughts and come up with a rational response		
Problem Solving Practice problem-solving strategies (articulate the problem, generate possible solutions, choose the best alternative) Break tasks down into manageable steps		
Relaxation Training Diaphragmatic breathing Progressive muscle relaxation		

Chapter 4   *Module 2: Adherence Training (Life-Steps)*

(Corresponds to chapter 3 of the workbook)

Materials Needed

- Client's completed CBT model of depression

- Adherence Goals Worksheet

- Reminder stickers for self-care cues

- Pillbox, if applicable

- Weekly Adherence Assessment Form

Outline

- Set agenda

- Review depression score on CES-D and discuss with client

- Review client's treatment adherence over the previous week

- Review material from previous module

- Conduct Life-Steps adherence intervention (see table 4.1 for outline of steps)

- Review all new plans

- Assign homework

  Therapist Note: It may be important to review the client's particular medical concerns before this session and obtain a familiarity with the types of adherence behaviors needed for his or her illness.

Table 4.1 Steps for Conducting Adherence Intervention

Step 1	Provide education, interactively, about adherence.
Step 2	Plan for transportation to medical appointments.
Step 3	Plan for optimizing communication with medical and mental health care providers.
Step 4	Plan for coping with side effects of medications and medical regimen.
Step 5	Plan for obtaining medications or other self-care items.
Step 6	Formulate a daily schedule for medication and other self-care behaviors (i.e., glucose monitoring for diabetic patients, exercise, etc.).
Step 7	Plan for storing medications.
Step 8	Develop cues for taking medications or implementing other self-care procedures (i.e., glucose monitoring).
Step 9	Prepare for adaptively coping with slips in adherence and preventing relapse.
Step 10	Review all plans.
Step 11	Make follow-up phone call (optional).

Because the Life-Steps intervention is composed of multiple steps, we have included a table outlining them for your use. You may refer to and use this table as a guide during sessions when conducting the intervention with clients. If you wish, you may photocopy the table from the book or download it from the Treatments *ThatWork*™ website at http://www.oup.com/us/ttw.

Set Agenda

In this module, setting the expectation that this particular session focuses on adherence and self-care behaviors allows the therapist and client to note additional emerging problems for future CBT sessions that more generally work on depression or life stress. We conceptualize this module as providing a foundation for future sessions in that it specifically addresses the adherence behaviors, whereas additional modules help treat depression in the context of attempting to maintain these adherence behaviors.

This module focuses on medical adherence and is based on a stand-alone, evidence-based, cognitive-behavioral and problem-solving intervention called Life-Steps (Safren et al., 1999). Although the self-care behaviors vary considerably from illness to illness (e.g., diabetes vs. HIV), the strategies described can be adapted to address a wide range of medical adherence behaviors as outlined in chapter 2. In the context of CBT-AD, we have adapted this intervention so that it is provided toward the beginning of the overall treatment after the general session on psychoeducation and motivational interviewing. Additional sessions of CBT-AD refer back to and integrate the adherence skills and goals identified in this module.

Because CBT-AD focuses on the integration of adherence enhancement with the treatment of depression, each of the following modules incorporates and reviews the adherence behaviors relevant to the particular client. As discussed in chapter 2, many medical conditions require significant behavioral changes that can be increasingly difficult if one suffers from comorbid depression. The specific medical condition and the adherence behaviors described in chapter 2 are discussed with the client during this session.

We recommend completing this module on adherence training in one session; however, for many clients, continued skills training is necessary, and future sessions can be devoted to review of this material. Subsequent modules on depression should also continue to incorporate the adherence material, particularly addressing avoidance of self-care behaviors as a behavioral component of depression.

Review of Depression Severity on CES-D

As in every session, the client completes the CES-D self-report measure of depression. Briefly review the score and take note of any symptoms that may have changed from the last measurement. Remember, as therapy progresses it can be helpful to review the total score for each of the preceding sessions in order to examine what might be helpful in treatment and what might not. Be sure to track scores using the Progress Summary Chart provided in the previous chapter.

Review of Adherence and Any Medical Changes

As always, the client completes the Weekly Adherence Assessment Form at the start of the session. Review the completed form and assess any medical changes since the last session, including changes in the client's symptoms, emergence of new symptoms, or any new test results. Use this review as an opportunity to provide feedback to the client and help him or her address any problems he or she is having with adherence. If necessary, renegotiate the planned medical regimen and adapt it to the client's needs.

Review of Previous Module

Remind the client that the previous session involved discussion of the cognitive, behavioral, and physical components of depression. Review the particular components for the client and remind him or her about how each of these three components interact, making it easier for depression and poor adherence and self-care to continue. We recommend referring back to the copy of the client's completed cognitive-behavioral model from the previous module (figure 3.2).

Remind the client that after this session that emphasizes adherence, the subsequent modules and sessions seek to interrupt this cycle, targeting both mental and physical health.

Sample questions for the client include:

- *What other questions do you have about the treatment we are going to begin?*

- *What questions do you have about how it applies to you?*

- *What else can you tell me that will help me structure the treatment to your situation?*

- *How has the past week been in terms of your thoughts, behaviors, and physical symptoms with respect to your mood and your ability to take care of your illness?*

- *What other thoughts do you have about your motivation to do this treatment?*

The point of these questions is to solidify credibility and confidence in the treatment. Specifically, point out how the cognitive-behavioral model directly applies to the client's concerns, and address any questions or issues that emerge.

After this discussion, remind the client that the topic of today's session is medical adherence and that future sessions will address depression more specifically. It is useful to describe self-care behaviors and adherence as a foundation for future sessions. You may use the following sample dialogue to accomplish this:

> *In future sessions we'll really be targeting your depression and working on skills to help with your mood. In today's session, we're going to start with making sure you have all the best skills to help you manage your illness. This is important for two reasons. First, making sure that you're doing everything you can to manage your illness is the best way to keep you physically healthy. Second, if you feel less overwhelmed by your self-care regimen—because you feel like you've developed a plan and have the skills to put that plan into practice—you will also likely*

feel less depressed. So, this is where we start, and we come back to these skills throughout this program. Does that plan make sense to you?

Utilize the CBT model of depression to discuss how the client's specific thoughts and behaviors may affect adherence and how this, in turn, affects the physical condition, which, in turn, can affect depression, continuing the cycle.

Life-Steps: Adherence and Self-Care Enhancement

Balance of Therapist Flexibility and Utilization of Specific Intervention Components

Although this module, as with the other modules, follows a specific format (setting an agenda, mood check using the CES-D, review of homework and previous material, introduction to the problem-solving steps for adherence), we also emphasize therapist flexibility. Some of the following self-care items will be relevant to some clients and illnesses, and others may be less relevant. Hence, each step should start with a brief discussion about the particular self-care behaviors required for the management of the client's illness, with more time spent on those self-care behaviors that are most problematic or important.

Chapter 2 contains an outline of the types of adherence behaviors needed for selected medical conditions that have strong adherence components. Information about the important adherence behaviors required for your client should be discussed here, depending on his or her particular medical condition. Additionally, using the client workbook, the therapist and the client can examine the particular adherence behaviors that will be targeted in this program.

The Need for Client "Buy In"

The first step of the adherence session involves a discussion of adherence in successful treatment of a medical condition. Providing an understandable rationale for the importance of self-care behaviors is a necessary (but not sufficient) component in helping a client make health-related behavioral changes. To help instill a sense of self-efficacy, we describe adherence as a skill that can be learned and utilize education as one component of this behavioral-change program.

Additionally, although many of the problem-solving steps for the adherence enhancement training stem from general principles of cognitive-behavioral therapy and also involve information, motivation, and behavioral skills training (Fisher & Fisher, 1992), the objectives are to elicit information about the client's current difficulties with adherence, incorporate them into the discussion of the model, and tailor the particular training materials to each particular client—making it directly relevant. Discussion of adherence in the context of the CBT model will also facilitate improving understanding of the relation of depression and adherence behaviors in hopes of further improving motivation to improve depression and adherence.

As with the subsequent treatment modules, we have found that the best way to present the rationale for Life-Steps within the context of CBT and tailoring it to the clients' needs is through an interactive discussion rather than a didactic presentation.

Whenever possible, consultation with the client's medical provider can enhance your ability to identify and prioritize important self-care behaviors given the client's current medical status. A collaborative relationship between the client, the client's physician, and the therapist is the ideal context for this treatment.

Suggested discussion points and sample dialogues follow.

The Purpose of This Module Is to Help With Adherence

The purpose of this module is to help you effectively follow the medical regimen prescribed by your doctor or other health care provider. For many people with a chronic medical condition, this involves regular use of medications. For others it also involves other challenging changes, such as following dietary restrictions, increasing exercise, monitoring of one's health using blood or other types of biological tests, and maintaining medical or mental health appointments.

Importance of Adherence

Self-care behaviors and medical adherence are an important part of the treatment of all chronic illnesses. Sometimes what you do at home and in your day-to-day life to manage your illness has a much bigger impact on your health than what happens in your doctor's office. For example, in diabetes, it's estimated that 95% of successful treatment depends on self-care behaviors. Research has shown that lifestyle changes for diabetes can be just as powerful as medications in preventing complications. For HIV, taking your medications on time as close to every time as possible is the best way to keep your viral load down and your CD4 cells up. For asthma, carrying your inhaler and taking your preventive medications regularly is the best way to avoid serious attacks. So, a lot of managing a chronic illness relies on what you do. That can be stressful for a lot of people, but it's also good news because it means that your health is under your control. In this program, we want to take as much of the stress of self-care as possible out of the picture and give you the skills necessary for medical adherence so that you can feel in control of your illness.

Taking Something That Seems Overwhelming and Making It Automatic

Many people, when first confronted with the number of new things needed to manage a complicated medical illness, can feel overwhelmed. Being able to manage your illness doesn't have to do with what kind of person you are. It's something that changes over time and depends on the skills and support you have to carry out your self-care regimen. The way you can think about it is that it can be a lot like learning to drive a car for the first time. First, you need to learn about all the steps and why they're important: how to hold the wheel, how much pressure to apply to the pedals, when to check your mirrors, and so forth. At first each one of these steps requires a lot of concentration and effort, but over time, they feel less like steps and more like automatic behaviors. As much as possible, we want to help you learn the skills necessary to manage your illness well enough so that you can incorporate them into your life in a way that makes them feel almost as automatic as all those steps involved in driving a car. Just like you learn the steps of driving a car because a car can take you places you want to go, learning the steps involved in managing your illness and following through with them is the best way you can get to better health.

Problem Solving

Problem-solving training refers to a general approach to training people to cope with stressful or overwhelming problems. One part of problem solving involves defining the problem and breaking it down into steps. A future module is dedicated to this general approach, but before that we are going to directly apply problem solving to medical adherence.

In problem solving, the first thing needed is to define the problem and articulate goals. So, that is where we will begin today.

Articulation of Adherence Goals: Review of Medical Illness Components

In order to have a basis for the material that follows, identify and discuss the medical adherence behaviors that are relevant to your client and collaboratively identify the particular adherence behaviors that will be targeted in this program.

With your help, the client will use the Adherence Goals worksheet in the corresponding workbook to write down a list of the self-care adherence behaviors that will be targeted during the subsequent steps. Sample completed forms for clients with two different chronic illnesses are provided in figures 4.1 and 4.2.

Refer to chapter 2 and review the relevant material for the specific illness that the client has. If the client has an illness that is not reviewed in this manual, use this part of the session to elicit adherence goals. Again, it is important to consult with the client's health care provider to understand what is most important for his or her health and to help formulate self-care/adherence goals.

Adherence Goals Worksheet

Name _____ Date _____

Generate a list of adherence/self-care goals and write them here.

Goal 1: _Monitor blood glucose twice a day_

Goal 2: _Take oral medications twice daily_

Goal 3: _Carry insulin and take as needed_

Goal 4: _Follow daily dietary recommendations_

Goal 5: _Exercise (cardio) for 30 minutes three times a week_

Figure 4.1.

Example of Completed List of Adherence Goals for Patient With Diabetes

Discuss each behavior and reinforce the client's understanding of adherence by summarizing the benefits of adherence and consequences of nonadherence. Also explain that adhering to his or her regimen is a skill that may be challenging to learn but can be done.

As you work with the client to formulate a plan and a backup plan for the adherence steps that follow, some information is needed from the client to more effectively tailor aspects of this intervention to his or her needs. You may ask your client the following questions in order to facilitate a discussion about barriers to and facilitators of adherence.

Before we start, what thoughts do you have regarding adherence to your medical regimen (i.e., taking pills, monitoring glucose)? What may get in the way of adhering to your regimen (i.e., schedule, forgetting, negative thoughts, depression, etc.)?

Example:

- *When do you usually tend to forget to take your medications (e.g., in the morning, at night, on weekends, when you go out)?*
- *How do you remember to take your medications (e.g., an alarm clock, take with breakfast or when doing another activity)?*
- *Do you sometimes feel so down that you do not feel like taking your medications?*

Adherence Goals Worksheet

Name _____ Date _____

Generate a list of adherence/self-care goals and write them here.

Goal 1: _Take my medications on time every day_ _____

Goal 2: _Schedule and attend medical visits every 3 months with my doctor_

Goal 3: _Remember to take Metamucil daily for side effects_ _____

Goal 4: _Exercise (lift weights) three times a week_ _____

Figure 4.2.

Example of Completed List of Adherence Goals for HIV-Infected Patient

When you look at your medications (or glucose monitor, etc.) what goes through your mind?

Probe for negative thinking to address as barriers to medication adherence and to later discuss during the module on cognitive restructuring. Examples of negative thoughts that can interfere with adherence and add to depression follow. (Note: workbook has space for client to list thoughts.)

1. The medication is going to make me feel sick (e.g., I will get a headache, feel nauseous).
2. The medications do not help me anyway so why bother?
3. The medications hurt me more than they help me.

What are your reasons for following this regimen (i.e., goals, family members, significant others)? What are your top five reasons for staying adherent and taking care of your medical illness? (Note: workbook has space for client to list reasons.)

Example:

1. I want to be alive for my daughter's graduation.
2. I want to be healthy enough to volunteer some of my time.
3. I want to be able to do my artwork once again.
4. I don't want to have to be hospitalized again.
5. I want to avoid additional medical complications.

Transition to Problem-Solving Steps

Introduce and explain the process of solving problems related to adherence. You may use the following sample dialogue:

We are now going to go through a list of problems that some people have with medical adherence. By addressing each problem related to adherence, solving it, and continuing to practice, you can make successful adherence a part of your routine.

We will use a technique called AIM to solve some of your adherence-related problems.

The first step of AIM is to:
- *Articulate the particular adherence goal.*

The second step is to:
- *Identify barriers to reaching the goal.*

The final step is to:
- *Make a plan to overcome the barriers, as well as to develop a backup plan.*

These steps are provided in outline form; however, each area is meant to be a discussion, with the client noting the goal, the barriers, and the plan for each in the spaces provided in the workbook.

Life-Steps

Life-Step 1: Getting to Appointments

This first step will help your client utilize problem-solving skills to help him or her identify measures that will facilitate getting to medical appointments.

AIM

1. Articulate the adherence goal regarding medical appointments.

   Suggested questions:
   - *How often do you have medical appointments?*
   - *Where do you go to have these medical appointments?*

2. Identify potential barriers:

   Suggested questions:
   - *What might cause you to miss appointments? (e.g., varying work schedules, work during clinic hours, children, long distance from clinic)*

3. Make a plan and a backup plan:

   Suggested questions:
   - *How will you get to your appointments in case the weather is bad or you can't go the way you usually go? (e.g., is there public transportation nearby, does clinic have a medical van for pickup, can you call and reschedule?)*
   - *How can you schedule them and make sure you remember?*

Develop a backup plan in case problems arise (e.g., schedule appointments early in the morning or later in the afternoon, go during lunch hour, know public transportation schedules in case other transportation fails).

Life-Step 2: Communicating With Treatment Team

Communication with one's medical provider can be a key component of treatment success. We have found that many clients have difficulties remembering questions to ask their provider, become nervous during medical visits, and forget information. It is important to discuss the issue of communication with the client and to come up with a plan that makes sense for the client in terms of meeting his or her goals at the next medical visit.

AIM

1. Articulate any questions or comments that the client would like to ask or discuss with his or her medical provider.

   Suggested questions:
   - *During your next visit with your doctor, what questions do you want to ask about your symptoms, medications, medication side effects, or recommended self-care behaviors (e.g., questions about diet, exercise)?*

2. Identify potential barriers to communication with the client's medical provider:

   Suggested questions:
   - *What might cause you to not ask your doctor the questions that you have (e.g., you feel uncomfortable talking about those symptoms; you always forget; your doctor just changed and you feel uncomfortable with the new doctor; your doctor is too busy to answer your questions)?*

3. Make a plan and a backup plan to overcome barriers:

   Suggested questions:
   - *How will you remember the questions that you want to ask your doctor?* (Suggest to the client that he or she write them down on an index card to bring to the medical visit.)
   - Rehearse/role-play with client about asking questions in order to:
     - Assess difficulties in communication
     - Address embarrassment/discomfort
     - Address irrational fears about asking questions
     - Help client to ask provider for full explanations in case providers seem too busy due to time pressures
   - After rehearsing, ask: *What other concerns do you have regarding being able to ask your questions of your doctor?*

Life-Step 3: Coping With Side Effects

Side effects are present in many treatment regimens and encompass an especially important area for client-provider communication and collaboration. There are many potential solutions to side effects, but many side effects have remedies that vary across illnesses. You can help the client to identify the side effects that are distressful to him or her and then ask the client to always consult with their physician about ways to manage them. The physician can further assess the side effects and identify strategies to address them. In collaboration with the client's physician, you can work with the client on using the strategies to manage the side effects. Also, it is important for clients to understand that in many cases, with medication adherence, side effects decrease over time so that they do not allow side effects to decrease medication adherence.

AIM

1. Articulate any problems with adherence that may emerge due to side effects.

   Suggested questions:
   - *What kinds of side effects do you have from your medications (e.g., headaches, nausea, muscle aches)?*
   - *Which medications do you think are causing these side effects?*

2. Identify potential barriers:

   Suggested questions:
   - *Have your side effects gotten in the way of taking your medications?*
   - *What have you done about the side effects so far? Have you been talking to your doctor about these side effects?*

3. Make a plan and a backup plan:

   Suggested questions:
   - *Will you be able to talk to your doctor about these side effects to see what else can be done to help you, like give you other medications or change these?*

- *In the meantime, do you think that you can continue to take the medications as prescribed until you speak to your doctor about them?*
- Refer to upcoming module on relaxation and diaphragmatic breathing, which can be helpful in coping with side effects.

Life-Step 4: Obtaining Medications and Other Relevant Health-Related Products

Encourage the client to work with his or her provider to develop a plan for continued access to medications or other products (i.e., monitoring devices). The plan should include information regarding payment options, pharmacy selection, backup plans for transportation or other issues, plans for refilling prescriptions, and management of client-pharmacist transactions.

AIM

1. Articulate the adherence goal of always having a sufficient supply of medications and needed supplies.

   Suggested questions:
   - *Where do you get your medications and medical supplies?*
   - *How do you pay for your medications and medical supplies?*
   - *How do you get to your pharmacy?*
   - *Have you ever run out of your medications or medical supplies?*
   - *When do you ask for a medication refill from your pharmacy?*
   - *When do you ask for a prescription refill from your doctor?*

2. Identify potential barriers:
   - *What might cause you to run out of your medications or other needed medical supplies?*
   - *What might get in the way of getting to your pharmacy?*

If the client identifies privacy/confidentiality concerns, role-play rehearsal (with cognitive restructuring) for requesting a private discussion with pharmacist.

■ *What might get in the way of getting another prescription from your doctor?*

3. Make a plan and a backup plan:
    ■ *How will you get to your pharmacy?*
    ■ *If there is bad weather, how will you get to your pharmacy?*
    ■ *Can you set up a medication mail-in so that your medications can be mailed to you directly?*
    ■ *How can you make sure that you do not run out of your medications?*
    ■ *How can you make sure that you do not run out of prescription refills?*

Life-Step 5: Formulating a Daily Medication Schedule

This step involves groundwork for cue-control strategies (see Life-Step 7) and additional problem-solving techniques to help clients to remember to take their medications. Review of medication schedule also allows for a chance to correct misunderstandings about the dosage schedules (such as need to keep daily exact dosage schedule if identified by medical provider).

Although the examples provided refer to taking medication as the self-care behavior, the same approach can be used to address other behaviors relevant to medical adherence, such as exercise, following dietary recommendations, monitoring blood glucose, and so forth. Therefore, given the particular needs of each client, you may cycle through this section several times, addressing various aspects of self-care separately (e.g., taking medications, engaging in exercise, following diet, etc.).

Using the Medical Regimen Schedule worksheet in the workbook, help the client complete a detailed map of an average day of taking medications and specify environmental and other cues for taking meds throughout the day. If medication adherence is problematic, it may be useful to use this worksheet for each day in the week or a weekday and a weekend. Information on the client's prescribed medication regimen and other adherence goals are found in the Weekly Adherence Assessment form and the Adherence Goals worksheet in the workbook. Use the Weekly Adherence Assessment to determine the ideal times and conditions (e.g., on an empty stomach vs. with food) for taking medications and completing other self-care activities. Also discuss variation in a "typical" schedule and include examples from weekend and holiday schedules. A sample completed worksheet is shown in figure 4.3.

AIM

1. Articulate the adherence goal of remembering to take medications/ follow medical regimen.

   Suggested questions:
   ▨ *When do you take your medications?*
   ▨ *How do you remember to take your medications?*
   ▨ *How often do you need to exercise?*
   ▨ *How often do you need to perform other self-management behaviors (e.g., self-monitoring of blood glucose)?*

2. Identify potential barriers:

   Suggested questions:
   ▨ *When do you tend to forget to take your medications? (Identify specific times that are potential risks for missing doses; e.g., weekends due to disruptions in routine.)*
   ▨ *Do you take your medications at a usual time when you are doing something else (like cup of coffee and toast in the morning; getting home from work; during nightly news)?*
   ▨ *What gets in the way of exercising regularly?*
   ▨ *What gets in the way of adhering to your diet?*

3. Make a plan and a backup plan:

   Suggested questions:
   ▨ *What activities can you do at the same time as you take your medication so that each time you do it, you will remember to take your medications, too (e.g., during breakfast, with an afternoon snack)?*
   ▨ *When would be the best times to schedule exercise?*
   ▨ *How can you be sure to follow what you need to with respect to diet?*

Medical Regimen Schedule

Day of the Week: Tuesday

Adherence Goals: Take all prescribed medications

                           Check glucose 3xs

                           Take 2 insulin doses

                           Increase physical activity

Time	Daily Activity	Adherence Goal
Morning		
6:30	Wake up & use bathroom	
7:00	Get dressed	Check glucose level and take insulin
7:30	Eat breakfast	
8:00	Drive to work	Take morning medications
9:00	Arrive at work	
10:00	Work	
11:00	Snack break	
Afternoon		
12:00	Work	
1:00	Lunch	Check glucose level after lunch
2:00–4:00	Work	
4:00	Snack break	
5:00	Leave work	
Evening		
6:00	Go to gym	Physical activity
7:00	Eat dinner	Take evening medications
8:00–10:00	Watch TV	Take insulin after dinner
10:00	Read the paper	Check glucose level
10:30	Go to bed	

Figure 4.3.

Example of Completed Medical Regimen Schedule

> ◼ *Backup plans: What if it is a raining and you had planned to walk outside? What if you forget to take your medications/ insulin?*

Life-Step 6: Storing Medications and Medical Supplies

Some medications require safe and portable storage or refrigeration, requiring problem-solving skills to address this issue.

AIM

1. Articulate the adherence goal of properly storing medications, even when not at home. For diabetes, carrying and storing glucose monitoring equipment, insulin, and syringe and needles may be of issue (particularly in the summer). For HIV, clients may wish to find private places to keep their medications.

   Suggested questions:
   - ◼ *If you leave home, do you take your medications (oral or injectable) with you if you know you will not be back in time for your dose?*
   - ◼ *How do you carry your medications (oral or injectable) or medical monitoring devices with you when you go out (e.g., do you keep them in a pillbox or a bag)?*

2. Identify potential barriers:

   Suggested questions:
   - ◼ *Where do you keep your medications when you go out and bring them with you?*
   - ◼ *Do any of your medications need to be refrigerated?*
   - ◼ *What will you do about storing medications when you are away from home?*

3. Make a plan and a backup plan:

   Suggested questions:

- If medications need to be refrigerated, ask: *What can you do instead of storing your medications in work or others' refrigerators? Suggest refrigerated lunch bag with an icepack instead?*
- *Let's take a look at your dose time again and see if you can take your doses in such a way that you will not have to worry about keeping your medication cold (this is to avoid refrigeration for medications that retain their potency for a number of hours).*
- *Would you be able to buy and use a small Ziplock bag or a pillbox for each dose of the day? That way you can mark each bag with the appropriate time you are supposed to take your medications and any other things you need to remember about them, like certain foods to eat or not eat with them and refrigeration information.*
- Suggest small bag for diabetes medical supplies (e.g., insulin or monitoring devices).
- Suggest having backups that are kept in the client's car trunk or glove compartment.

Life-Step 7: Cue-Control Strategies for Taking Medications

This step can help clients learn strategies for remembering to take medications and for rehearsing adaptive thoughts of adherence each time they look at the cues.

Introduce the client to a system for reminding him- or herself to take medications. Round, colored adhesive stickers can be placed in or around the home or workplace as reminder strategies. The client should also place a sticker on a note card and write on the card a particular issue he or she wants to be reminded of when he or she sees the reminder stickers elsewhere (e.g., "Remember, I am taking my pills because I want to be healthy for my grandchildren"). This provides a link between the adaptive thoughts identified in Life-Step 1 and the dots in the client's environment.

AIM

1. Articulate the adherence goal of using strategies to improve motivation for and to remember to take medications.

   Suggested questions:
   ▨ *How do you usually help remind yourself to take your medications?*
   ▨ *What do you think about when you know it is time to take your medications?*

2. Identify potential barriers:

   Suggested questions:
   ▨ *What things do you think may keep you from using the dots? Do you think the dots would be helpful reminders of taking your medications?*

3. Make a plan and a backup plan:

   Suggested questions:
   ▨ *Where can you place each dot so that you can see it at each dosing time (e.g., near doorknob inside the house, near lock outside door, bathroom mirror, work computer, phone receiver, or other helpful places)?*
   ▨ *What other things do you think you can use to help you remember your medications (e.g., link taking medications with trips to the bathroom upon awakening and before going to bed, pillboxes with built-in timer alarms, wake-up call service, clocks or timers that chime on the hour or half-hour, and use of computers to sound alarms at designated times)?*

Life-Step 8: Handling Slips in Adherence

This step may help clients to prepare to recover from missing doses, lapsing from an exercise routine, or breaking their diet regimen, which, in the long run, is likely to occur. If a lapse occurs, the best choice is to return to one's adherence program as soon as possible instead of acting on hopeless thoughts and giving up. Identifying what led to the lapse can provide important information that can help solidify the skills and avoid future lapses. It should be stressed that lapses are normal and not a big problem. They only become a big problem when they lead to relapse and giving up on the self-care regimen.

Many clients feel that progress in behavioral change will be linear. However, in behavioral-change programs, progress actually happens in the context of the normal ups and downs of life. Hence, there will be good days and bad days. A discussion of the graph shown in figure 4.4 can help clients to improve their expectations about what behavioral change really looks like. Point to the graph and discuss how most clients expect change to happen steadily and consistently in contrast to how progress usually happens, with its ebbs and flows over the sessions. At times in treatment, clients may experience a worsening of symptoms or a lapse in their ability to employ behavioral skills. Instead of reacting to these as failures, these are opportunities to gather information about what contributed to the negative change and to allow new learning. It is impor-

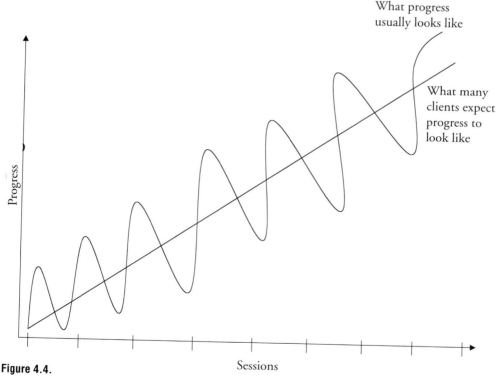

Figure 4.4.

Improvement Graph

tant for the therapist to normalize these lapses. Over the long run, successfully dealing with these short-term lapses will help clients be able to maintain treatment outcomes.

AIM

1. Articulate the adherence goal of understanding that making a change takes time and practice—slips can happen.

    Suggested questions:
    - *How would you feel if one day you forget to take your medications or sleep through the time for them or are sick and do not feel like taking them?*
    - *How would you feel if one day you don't follow through with an exercise or diet plan that you had set for yourself?*
    - *What would you do if that happens?*

2. Identify potential barriers:

    Suggested questions:
    - *What kinds of thoughts do you think may keep you from restarting your medical regimen if you have a slip?*

3. Make a plan and a backup plan:

    Suggested questions:
    - *What can you do to pick yourself up and start where you left off before you had a slip?* (Encourage clients to avoid all-or-nothing thinking when a slip occurs.)
    - *What can you learn from a lapse that will help you avoid another in the future?*

Review of Procedures

Review the previous steps and assess whether the client has understood the rationale behind each one. Doing this can help the client remember the strategies discussed during the session. Have the client write out any action items in the space provided in the workbook (e.g., questions to ask physician, placing the colored dots, and purchasing a refrigerator bag, pillbox, or an alarm watch/clock). Ask the client if he or she has any questions or concerns.

Is there anything else that may get in the way of your doing any of the steps that we just reviewed?

Lastly, review the specifics of the plan and backup plan for each of the adherence steps discussed.

Follow-Up (Optional)

You may schedule a follow-up phone call with the client before your next session to review strategies and cues specified during the session, to assess the emergence of any new problems/barriers and explore alternative solutions, and to determine whether additional sessions focused on adherence are needed.

Homework

For this module, the homework is inherent in each of the steps previously described. During the review, the therapist and client go over all of the particular action items for the client for the next session. Remind the client that this session covered adherence to medical regimens and that future sessions will begin the work that targets depression and integrates treating depression with self-care.

Chapter 5 | *Module 3: Activity Scheduling*

(Corresponds to chapter 4 of the workbook)

Materials Needed

- Positive Events Checklist
- Activity Log

Outline

- Set agenda
- Review depression score on CES-D and discuss with client
- Review client's treatment adherence over the previous week and problem-solve any emerging difficulties or slips
- Review material and homework from previous modules
- Introduce activity scheduling
- Work with client to identify pleasurable activities
- Assign homework

Set Agenda

The purpose of this module is to help clients activate themselves. A key behavioral component of depression is the absence of pleasurable events. During this session, clients will learn to identify times and situations when they are more and less likely to feel depressed. Despite chronic illness, it is important, with respect to managing mood, to be engaged in enjoyable activities. Clients will use the Positive Events Checklist in the workbook to identify activities that involve pleasure or mastery.

It is estimated that it will take one session to lay the groundwork for activity scheduling but that activity scheduling will be a part of future sessions on cognitive restructuring. Some individuals will require additional sessions to learn about pacing. This can be done as part of additional modules or can involve dedicating full sessions to reviewing activities, pacing suggestions, and overcoming barriers to activities. Note, however, that the problem-solving and cognitive restructuring modules are forthcoming, so if extensive problem-solving is required or if negative thoughts are barriers to activity scheduling, it may be important to complete those modules first and then return to activity scheduling.

Review of Depression Severity on CES-D

As in every session, the client completes the CES-D self-report measure of depression. Briefly review the score and take note of any symptoms that may have changed from the last measurement. Remember, as therapy progresses it can be helpful to review the total score for each of the preceding sessions in order to examine what might be helpful in treatment and what might not. Be sure to track scores using the Progress Summary Chart provided in chapter 3.

Review of Adherence and Any Medical Changes

The client also completes the Weekly Adherence Assessment Form. This form is included in the corresponding client workbook. Be sure to assess any medical changes since the last session, including changes in symptoms or emergence of new symptoms, or new test results. Also review the relation of these medical changes to adherence behavior and correlation with mood.

Review of Previous Modules and Homework

Review: CBT Model of Depression

Review the model with the client and remind him or her of the cognitive, behavioral, and physical components of depression and how they interact, making it easier for depression and poor adherence and poor self-care to continue. This can be used as a setup for the present module, stating that the goal, after review, is to attack the behavioral component of depression. If necessary, refer back to the copy of the client's completed CBT model from chapter 3.

Review: Life-Steps

Remind the client that the last session focused on learning how to effectively follow the medical regimen prescribed by his or her doctor or other health care provider. Review the importance of self-care behaviors and medical adherence, as well as the problem-solving technique (AIM) demonstrated in the previous session. Make additional plans or backup plans for any new strategy that did not work out.

Activity Scheduling

Introduce activity scheduling by referring back to the cognitive-behavioral model of depression discussed in chapter 3. Remind the client that the behavioral component of depression refers to the particular behaviors that he or she does or does not do because of depression. The client may be avoiding situations that normally provide him or her with pleasure or make him or her feel competent. If the client does not engage in pleasurable activities however, depression may increase.

Be sure to address the possibility that the client may not be able to participate in enjoyable activities because of the physical limitations of his or her illness (e.g., an asthmatic client who can't engage in physical exercise such as hiking or jogging). Work with the client to brainstorm alternative options (e.g., going for a short walk in the evenings around the neighborhood). Additionally, problem solving for medication taking or other aspects of self-care should be appropriately integrated into the elicitation of potential positive events to engage in by clients with a medical illness.

Positive Events Checklist

Using the Positive Events Checklist, work with the client to create a list of events that he or she no longer does but used to do before becoming depressed and/or chronically ill. The goal of this exercise is to identify activities that the client can begin to participate in once again that will make him or her feel more positive and that can be done in conjunction with the limitations of a chronic illness.

We recommend going over the entire list with the client in the session. The reason is that, in our experience, clients with depression seem to quickly jump to the conclusion that they do not have any interests or that any interests they do have will not be possible to do now that they are ill. We find that a discussion of each and every item in the list ends up helping with client rapport and helps a discussion of a large number of simple and more involved activities that the client can do as hobbies or pleasurable activities during the day.

We also recommend helping clients, throughout the remainder of the treatment, to stay engaged in regularly occurring positive activities. Hence, future modules all include checking back with clients regarding the material presented in this module. Ideally, clients can learn about some new type of regularly occurring activity that they can participate in so that they can see and meet new people on a regular basis. For example, if a person has a pet, he or she can go to the same park every day when the park is full and eventually meet the other pet owners. If the person is interested in art, potentially he or she can join an art group that meets weekly or monthly. Scheduling medication taking and other self-care activities should be part of the discussion—to problem-solve ways around these activities.

It is also important to set appropriate expectations regarding reengaging in these activities. For example, if the client has the goal of meeting new friends by joining a club, he or she cannot expect to have new friends after the first or second event. However, if the client goes to a regularly occurring activity, it is likely that over time he or she will see some of the same people and slowly get to know them and establish relationships.

Activity Log

The goals of the activity log are for the client (1) to learn firsthand the association of mood symptoms to activities and (2) to gain a sense of his or her limits in terms of his or her physical symptoms. Understanding the association of mood and activities may be much more effective than recall, because individuals with depression tend to view their previous week consistently with their mood state. This can result in a belief that the entire week was negative, when, in fact, clients, through monitoring, can learn that there are some parts of the week that are actually enjoyable. This can then be a baseline for decreasing more depressogenic activities and increasing activities that promote positive affect.

Regarding their limits for pacing, it is important to monitor symptoms of their illness so that the frequency and quality of positive activities can be maximized. Living with a chronic illness may mean that the client may not be able to do everything that he or she wants to do. For example, a client who suffers from fatigue may be better off resting the day before his or her daughter's soccer game to have enough energy to attend. The client may also need to plan to rest the day after the game, as he or she will likely be tired. Having the expectation of symptoms based on one's previous pattern can allow you and the client both to minimize the degree to which symptomatic "flare-ups" arise in an unexpected or unpredictable way and to develop a plan to prevent and treat such flare-ups.

The client will begin using the Activity Log in the workbook to monitor daily activities (what he or she is doing during the relevant time periods, what his or her mood is like during those times, and any medical symptoms experienced during those times). Instruct the client to also select the most prominent medical symptom of his or her illness to moni-

Table 5.1. Positive Events Checklist

1. Going to lunch with a friend
2. Speaking to a friend on the telephone
3. Going to a movie
4. Relaxing in a park or backyard
5. Reading a book for pleasure
6. Going for a walk with a friend or partner
7. Going out for ice cream or sugar-free frozen yogurt on a warm evening
8. Attending a play or show
9. Playing a game with a child or friend
10. Having a special meal or treat
11. Taking a bubble bath
12. Creating art on your computer
13. Building or upgrading a computer
14. Taking digital photos
15. Baking
16. Creating glass art
17. Organizing pictures
18. Helping other people
19. Volunteering
20. Cooking a gourmet meal
21. Renting a movie
22. Making jewelry
23. Getting a manicure or pedicure
24. Rollerblading
25. Getting involved in your community
26. Donating money to the charity of your choice
27. Joining a gym
28. Playing bocce, racquetball, or squash
29. Snowshoeing
30. Kayaking
31. Redecorating your home
32. Getting a pet (or playing with someone else's dog or cat)
33. Mountain biking
34. Apple picking
35. Weightlifting
36. Playing chess or other board games
37. Going to a comedy club
38. Playing golf / miniature golf
39. Going to the driving range
40. Curling
41. Playing Frisbee
42. Telling jokes and funny stories
43. People watching
44. Going window shopping
45. Stargazing
46. Rock climbing (indoor climbing wall)
47. Blowing bubbles
48. Going to a toy store
49. Bird watching
50. Going on a nature walk
51. Having a cup of tea
52. Playing cards with friends / establishing a "poker night"
53. Going to an arcade
54. Surfing the Internet
55. Downloading songs to your MP3 player
56. Chatting online
57. Watching TV
58. Using TiVo or DVR to record your favorite shows
59. Playing video games online
60. Starting a collection (stamps, coins, shells, etc.)
61. Going on a date
62. Relaxing
63. Jogging, walking, running
64. Thinking I have done a full day's work
65. Listening to music
66. Recalling fond memories
67. Going shopping
68. Lying in the sun
69. Laughing
70. Reading magazines or newspapers
71. Hobbies (model building, scrapbook making, etc.)
72. Spending an evening with good friends
73. Planning a day's activities
74. Meeting new people
75. Eating healthful foods
76. Practicing karate, judo, kickboxing
77. Thinking about retirement
78. Tackling home improvement projects
79. Repairing things around the house
80. Working on car or bicycle or motorcycle
81. Wearing sexy clothes
82. Having quiet evenings
83. Taking care of my plants
84. Buying, selling stock
85. Swimming
86. Doodling, drawing, painting
87. Exercising
88. Going to a party
89. Playing soccer
90. Flying kites
91. Having discussions with friends
92. Having family get-togethers
93. Having safe sex
94. Going camping
95. Singing
96. Arranging flowers
97. Practicing religion (going to church, group praying, etc.)
98. Going to the beach
99. Having class reunions
100. Going skating
101. Going sailboating

102. Planning a trip or vacation
103. Doing something spontaneous
104. Doing needlepoint, crocheting, or knitting
105. Going on a scenic drive
106. Entertaining / having a party
107. Joining a social club (e.g., garden club, Parents without Partners, etc.)
108. Flirting / kissing
109. Playing musical instruments
110. Doing arts and crafts
111. Making a gift for someone
112. Buying music (records, CDs, etc.)
113. Watching sports on television
114. Cooking
115. Going on a hike
116. Writing
117. Buying clothes
118. Going out to dinner
119. Discussing books / joining a book club
120. Sightseeing
121. Gardening
122. Going to a spa
123. Going out for coffee
124. Playing tennis
125. Doing yoga / stretching
126. Being with / playing with children
127. Going to concerts
128. Planning to go to school
129. Refinishing furniture
130. Going bike riding
131. Buying gifts
132. Traveling to national parks
133. Going to a spectator sport (auto racing, horse racing, etc.)
134. Teaching
135. Fishing
136. Playing with animals
137. Acting
138. Writing in a journal
139. Writing and sending letters or e-mails
140. Cleaning
141. Taking an exercise class
142. Watching comedy
143. Taking a class
144. Learning a new language
145. Doing crossword puzzles, word jumbles, playing Sudoku
146. Performing magic tricks
147. Getting a new haircut
148. Going to a stylist
149. Going to a bookstore
150. Buying books
151. Dancing
152. Going on a picnic
153. Meditating
154. Playing volleyball
155. Going to the mountains
156. Splurging / treating yourself
157. Having a political discussion
158. Playing softball
159. Seeing and/or showing photos or slides
160. Playing pool
161. Dressing up and looking nice
162. Reflecting on how I've improved
163. Talking on the phone
164. Going to museums
165. Lighting candles
166. Listening to the radio
167. Getting a massage
168. Saying "I love you"
169. Thinking about my good qualities
170. Taking a sauna or a steam bath
171. Skiing (cross-country or downhill)
172. Whitewater rafting
173. Bowling
174. Woodworking
175. Taking dance classes (ballet, tap, salsa, ballroom, etc.)
176. Sitting in a sidewalk café
177. Having an aquarium
178. Erotica (sex books, movies)
179. Horseback riding
180. Doing something new
181. Doing jigsaw puzzles
182. Thinking I'm a person who can cope
183. Going sledding
184. Going to the mall
185. Making a home video

Adapted from Hickling & Blanchard, 2006; Linehan et al., 1993; and from brainstorming of the authors and colleagues.

Activity Log

Rate activities for mood (1-10). 1 = bad mood, 10 = best mood.

	Monday	Tuesday	Wednesday	Thursday	Friday	Saturday	Sunday
Morning	Went to bank-2 Dr. visit-5 Exercised-4	Slept late, stayed in bed, watched TV-2	Bed/TV-2	Read a book-6 Had coffee-4	Watched TV-4	Exercised while listening to music-8 Watched TV-4	Had a nice brunch-5
Afternoon	Took a ride with a friend who is courier all over Eastern Mass-8	Mostly watched TV, hung around the house, used the Internet-2	Hung around the house, used the Internet, watched TV-2	Went out for the afternoon: Visited book-store-8 Read outside of bookstore-8 Walked around the stores-7	My sister Kathy came by with card for me-8 Talked on phone with a friend-7 Had coffee-5	Went to store-6 Walked to park and read-8	Kathy picked me up and we went to my sister's-8
Evening	Watched TV-4 Took bills to my sister's-4	Watched TV-4	Dinner at my sister's house-8	Cleaned shelves and back hall-6 Watched TV-4	Watched TV-4	Watched TV-4	Dinner party with my sisters for my birthday-8

Figure 5.1.

Example of Completed Activity Log

tor (e.g., if fatigue is a concern, rate level of fatigue; if pain is a concern, rate level of pain). If the client does not experience symptoms, he or she should enter a "0" as the daily symptom rating. Clients with diabetes should also use the log to record their glucose levels.

A sample, filled-out Activity Log is shown in figure 5.1.

Homework

✎ Client should continue practicing adherence skills from his or her adherence action item list.

✎ Instruct the client to begin incorporating pleasant activities into his or her daily schedule (ideally, make a specific goal with the client of specific activities to try, or a goal such as "do at least one pleasant activity per day").

✎ Client should monitor activity and mood levels on a daily basis using the Activity Log in the workbook.

Chapter 6 *Module 4: Cognitive Restructuring (Adaptive Thinking)*

(Corresponds to chapters 5 and 6 of the workbook)

COGNITIVE RESTRUCTURING *Part I*

Materials Needed

▨ Preliminary Instructions for Cognitive Restructuring

▨ Cognitive Distortions List

▨ Thought Record

Outline

▨ Set agenda

▨ Review depression score on CES-D and discuss with client

▨ Review client's treatment adherence over the previous week and problem-solve any emerging difficulties or slips

▨ Review material and homework from previous modules

▨ Explain the technique of cognitive restructuring

▨ Discuss cognitive distortions and automatic thoughts

▨ Introduce the 4-Column Thought Record and show client how to use it to monitor automatic thoughts and cognitive distortions

▨ Assign homework

Set Agenda

It is estimated that it will take approximately five sessions to deliver the information in this module. The first two sessions will be used to train the client in the technique of cognitive restructuring. The therapist will teach the client adaptive thinking skills for depression and living with a chronic illness. The remaining sessions will focus on rehearsing and practicing the skills learned and integrating cognitive restructuring with activity scheduling and self-care/medication adherence.

Review of Depression Severity on CES-D

As in every session, the client completes the CES-D self-report measure of depression. Briefly review the score and take note of any symptoms that may have changed from the last measurement. Remember, as therapy progresses it can be helpful to review the total score for each of the preceding sessions in order to examine what might be helpful in treatment and what might not. Be sure to track scores using the Progress Summary Chart provided in chapter 3.

Review of Adherence and Any Medical Changes

The client also completes the Weekly Adherence Assessment Form. Be sure to assess any medical changes since the last session, including changes in symptoms or emergence of new symptoms, or new test results. Also review the relation of these medical changes to adherence behavior and correlation with mood. When reviewing the adherence form, it is important to make a plan and a backup plan for any slips in adherence from the previous week.

Review of Previous Modules and Homework

Review: CBT Model of Depression

Review the model with the client and remind him or her of the cognitive, behavioral, and physical components of depression and how they interact, making it easier for depression and poor adherence and poor self-care to continue. If necessary, refer back to the copy of the client's completed CBT model from chapter 3. Use this as an introduction to the current module, which focuses on the cognitive component of depression.

Review: Life-Steps

Remind client about how to effectively follow the medical regimen prescribed by his or her doctor or other health care provider. Review the importance of self-care behaviors and medical adherence, as well as the problem-solving technique (AIM). Make additional plans or backup plans for any new strategy that did not work out.

Review: Activity Scheduling

Spend time carefully reviewing activity scheduling, using the client's completed Activity Log for the previous week to point out times when his or her mood was elevated and times when his or her mood was depressed. Use this as a justification to maximize pleasurable activities. Look for any patterns with respect to symptoms (or, for diabetic patients, glucose levels) and their relationship to mood, and make a corrective action plan as needed.

Cognitive Restructuring

We have split the cognitive restructuring information into two parts, with the first focusing on identifying automatic thoughts and matching them to cognitive distortions. Preliminary instructions for cognitive restructuring are provided for the client in the workbook. We have also included them here as a reference. The information that follows loosely corresponds to the instruction sheet. While you go over this material, the client can follow along in the workbook.

Preliminary Instructions for Cognitive Restructuring

The purpose of using Thought Records is to identify and modify negative automatic thoughts in situations that lead to feeling overwhelmed.

The first step in learning to think in more useful ways is to become more aware of these thoughts and their relationship to your feelings. If you are anticipating a stressful situation or a task that is making you feel overwhelmed, write out your thoughts regarding this situation.

If a situation has already passed and you find that you are thinking about it negatively, list your thoughts for this situation.

*The **first column** of the Thought Record is for you to provide a description of the situation.*

*The **second column** is for you to list your thoughts during a stressful, overwhelming, or uncontrollable situation.*

*The **third column** is for you to write down what emotions you are having and what your mood is like when you are thinking these thoughts (e.g., depressed, sad, angry).*

*The **fourth column** is for you to see whether your thoughts match the list of "cognitive distortions." These may include:*

- *All-or-nothing thinking*

- *Overgeneralizations*

- *Jumping to conclusions: Fortune-telling/mind reading*

- *Magnification/minimization*

- *Emotional reasoning*

- *"Should" statements*

- *Labeling and mislabeling*

- *Personalization*

- *Maladaptive thinking*

Introduce the concept of cognitive restructuring by once again referring to the cognitive-behavioral model of depression from chapter 3. The cognitive component consists of negative thoughts that people have when they are depressed. Cognitive restructuring is a way to change these negative thoughts and beliefs in an effort to relieve depression.

It is important to note that cognitive restructuring is different from "positive thinking." Positive thinking would be arbitrarily replacing negative thoughts with positive thoughts. The goal of cognitive restructuring is to come up with alternative thoughts that are true and realistic and that make one feel better. This is particularly important for living with chronic illness because many of the stressors clients experience are real— and hence appraisals and cognitive restructuring techniques should involve realistic ways of thinking about situations that can objectively be negative (i.e., worsening of a prognosis; the real threat, for example, with HIV, that one can become resistant to one's medications).

Cognitive restructuring can also help with activity scheduling. Using the client's completed Activity Log from the previous week, point out times when he or she rated his or her mood the lowest and how cognitive restructuring could have been used to increase it. For example, we had a client who went to church for the first time in several years. She had previously avoided church because she felt that people would judge her for having HIV because it can be transmitted sexually. She arrived right as the service began, sat in the back, and walked right out when it was over. She rated her mood as low in this situation, with the interpretation that even in church, where one would think people would be friendly, she was not able to make friends. She took it personally that no one spoke to her. The realistic cognitive restructuring involved looking at the situation more objectively, with the interpretation that maybe no one spoke to her because there was not much time to do so. This resulted in the goal of arriving early and staying late to the next service, trying this three times, and seeing whether she would participate in any conversations.

Cognitive Distortions

Have the client turn to the Cognitive Distortions List in the workbook. Help the client identify which types of thoughts seem to apply to him or her most. Explain to the client that cognitive distortions maintain negative thinking and help to maintain negative emotions. Point out that negative and inaccurate thoughts and beliefs can lead to adverse behavioral consequences, including avoidance, feelings of helplessness and hopelessness, depression, the inability to take adequate care of oneself, and poor adherence to medications. Refer back to the client's completed CBT model of depression as needed.

We recommend going through the list of cognitive distortions individually with clients and asking for specific examples of times when they think they have had the various types of thoughts here. If a client does have difficulty, it can be useful to return to the CBT model of depression from chapter 3, in which the therapist and client had elicited negative thoughts or beliefs related to depression and illness.

List of Cognitive Distortions

All-or-nothing thinking: You see things in black-and-white categories. For example, you have to change your *entire life* because you are taking medicines for your illness, or *all* aspects of a project need to be completed immediately, or if your performance falls short of perfect, you see it as a total failure. For example, you are trying to eat a healthy diet but one day you "slip up" and overeat something you know is not healthy. The next day, you say to yourself, "Either I stick to my diet or it's no use! Since I messed up yesterday, it doesn't matter what I eat today, the rest of the weekend, or the rest of the month."

Overgeneralization: You see a single negative event as a never-ending pattern. You have a low blood sugar count (or maybe a really high one) after you've been trying to make some changes to your diet and exercise, and you say to yourself, "I'm never going to be able to get my diabetes in control! What I do makes no difference and I'm just no good at taking care of myself. Nothing will ever change anyway!"

Mental filter: You pick out a single negative detail and dwell on it exclusively, so that your vision of all reality becomes darkened, like the drop of ink that discolors the entire beaker of water. For example, you are working on increasing your glucose monitoring and physical activity and trying to eat a better daily diet. Although this has been going well and you've made consistent improvements, you only focus on the negatives. For example, you might think, "Well, yeah, I've been trying but it's not going to make any difference because I haven't lost weight yet." You focus on negative information and ignore all the positives.

Disqualifying the positive: You reject positive experiences or successes by insisting they "don't count" for one reason or another. In this way, you can maintain a negative belief that is contradicted by your everyday experiences. For example, when someone gives you a compliment, maybe you say to yourself, "They are just being nice." For instance, if someone compliments your clothes, you say, "Oh, this old thing?" This is a destructive negative thought because what you are telling yourself is that you are second-rate and not worth the compliment. Instead, you can choose to accept the positive and when someone compliments you, say, "Thank you!" You might even think, "How nice of them to notice," because you have already focused on your positive qualities.

Jumping to conclusions: You make a negative interpretation even though there are no facts that convincingly support your conclusion.

> *Mind reading*: You arbitrarily conclude that someone is reacting negatively to you, and you don't bother to check this out. For example, you assume that the person you are attracted to knows you are HIV-infected and therefore will not want to date you.

> *Fortune-telling*: You anticipate that things will turn out badly, and you feel that your prediction is a predetermined fact. For example, you predict that no matter what you do, you will never lose the weight you need to in order to stay healthy.

Magnification/minimization: You exaggerate the importance of things (such as the degree to which your illness affects a situation, your life, or other people; your mistakes; or someone else's achievement) or you inappropriately shrink things until they appear tiny (your own desirable qualities; your ability to do something despite having a chronic illness; or the other's imperfections).

Catastrophizing: You attribute extreme and horrible consequences to the outcomes of events. For example, you might interpret one slip with medications or monitoring as meaning that you will never be able to manage your regimen. One mistake at work = being fired from your job; one bad day = you will be unhappy forever.

Emotional reasoning: You assume that your negative emotions necessarily reflect the way things really are: "I feel it, so it must be true." "I feel bad about myself for being overweight, and therefore other people will think I am a bad person." Another example might be, "I feel guilty, so I deserve this" or "I feel depressed, so I must be a loser."

"Should" statements: You try to motivate yourself with "shoulds" and "shouldn'ts," as if you need to be punished before you could be expected to do anything. When you direct "should" statements toward others, you feel anger, frustration, and resentment. For example, you believe that you "should" clean the house every day, but you do not have the time to do it, and then you feel guilty.

Labeling and mislabeling: This is an extreme form of overgeneralization. Instead of describing an error, you attach a negative label to yourself or others. For example, you may forget to take your medications and say to yourself, "I'm stupid" or "I'm no good at this."

Personalization: You see negative events as indicative of some negative characteristic of yourself or others, or you take responsibility for events that were not your doing. Your significant other might come home in a bad mood after work, and you might say to yourself, "she/he is mad at me," or, "she/he doesn't even care about me anymore."

Maladaptive thinking: You focus on a thought that may be true but over which you have no control (e.g., "my abilities are more limited than they were before I was sick"). Excessively thinking about it can be self-critical or can distract you from an important task or from attempting new behaviors.

This list is from Heimberg (1991), with some modifications. Heimberg (1991) was originally based on Burns (1980) and Persons (1989).

Automatic thoughts (ATs) are thoughts that "automatically" come to mind when a particular situation occurs. Instead of reacting to the reality of a situation, an individual reacts to his or her own distorted viewpoint of the situation. Explain to the client that when he or she is depressed, automatic thoughts are more likely to be negative in nature. Ask the client if he or she has learned to drive a car. If yes, then use the following example to illustrate the concept of automatic thinking to the client:

Think about when you first learned to drive a car. At the age of 15 or 16, trying to coordinate many tasks at once, you had to be specifically conscious of handling the steering wheel, remembering to signal for turns, staying exactly in your lane, averting other traffic, trying to park, and doing many tasks at the same time that required your total attention.

Now, think about driving today. You probably know how to drive without thinking actively about what you are doing. The process of driving has become automatic.

In the same way that driving has become automatic, so can one's interpretation of various situations, which can result in a continuation of depressed mood. People tend to automatically interpret situations consistent with their moods. So, if someone is depressed for a prolonged period of time, the person continues to interpret neutral or even positive situations in ways that are consistent with their negative view of themselves, the future, and the past. For example, we had a client with diabetes who was overweight and had depression. She maintained the belief that she was ugly and that therefore no one would want to talk with her or be her friend. When she would go to events she would not approach new people or talk to them. When people would approach her, she would shy away from maintaining a conversation because of this negative view of herself. This pattern of thinking and behavior became automatic—and reinforced itself— because, in the end, it became a self-fulfilling prophecy. People did not speak to her because she avoided them due to her thoughts and beliefs about herself.

Identifying Automatic Thoughts

Using the Thought Record in the workbook, explain to the client how to monitor his or her thoughts. Have the client pick a situation from his or her completed Activity Log that rated as being a low point from the previous week and elicit automatic thoughts from the situation (if the client did not complete an activity log, try to help him or her elicit a situation from memory by asking questions like, *In thinking about the past week, what was the time or times when your mood was at its worst?*) As your discussion continues, you and the client can list these automatic thoughts on the Thought Record. The last column of the Thought Record will be left blank for now, as rational responses have yet to be discussed. A sample completed Thought Record without rational responses is shown in figure 6.1.

Teaching clients how to identify automatic thoughts can be a time-consuming and difficult process. A potential pitfall for therapists in the cognitive restructuring module would be to neglect a thorough elicitation of the full set of thoughts behind a client's interpretation of an event that made him or her upset. At first, the discussion may not address the core of the problem, but asking questions to start the dialogue can lead to a fuller and more intense therapeutic discourse.

Additionally, one needs to pay specific attention to thoughts related to a medical illness. Patients with a medical condition can "internalize" thoughts and beliefs about themselves consistent with being a "sick person," which can color their interpretation of situations and events.

Beginning questions can include:

- *What was going on in your head right then?*

- *What were you thinking when this happened?*

- *What was it about the situation that, specifically, made you upset?*

These questions typically elicit superficial, but negative, thoughts that are focused on the situation itself. This may be the focus in beginning sessions or, for some clients, throughout the treatment. However, further questioning (discussed in more detail in part II of the cognitive restructuring section) can reveal deeper "beliefs" behind the thoughts.

Thought Record

Time and situation	Automatic thoughts (what was going through your head?)	Mood and intensity of mood (0–100)	Cognitive distortions (match thoughts from list)	Rational response
Tues. afternoon: Went to cookout with my girlfriend and daughter.	Good memories (at first) of wife who passed away.	First, felt really good (80)		
	I don't take care of myself well enough.	A little sad (60)	"Should" thinking	
	Because of this, I won't live long enough to have these kinds of outings to enjoy with my family.	Very sad and guilty (95)	Fortune-telling "Should" thinking	
	My daughter lost her mother and has a horrible father.		Labeling	
Weds. morning: I woke up and knew it was time to take my medications but I had to push myself to get out of bed and so I just didn't take them.	I'm never going to be healthy. I can't take care of myself. I am a horrible person.	Disappointed in myself (80) Hopeless (95)	Catastrophizing Labeling	

Figure 6.1.

Example of Completed Thought Record Up to Cognitive Distortions Column

Questioning ways to get beyond the negative thoughts specific to that situation can allow a deeper understanding of an ongoing pattern of interpreting situations negatively. Many times, for example, negative beliefs emerge that tie one's identity into one's illness. Other times, beliefs emerge that were present before the illness but have become exacerbated. Identifying negative beliefs can help clients look toward future situations or thinking patterns in order to make longer lasting changes. Probes for eliciting these beliefs may include:

- *Why do you think you saw it that way?*

- *What does that say about you?*

- *What would make you interpret the situation in the way that you just described?*

- *Can you think of the first time you thought that way about something like this?*

- *Has your thinking about situations like this changed since you became chronically ill?*

Identifying Cognitive Distortions

Once automatic thoughts have been identified, one way of helping a client with depression and a chronic illness think more adaptively can be to have him or her match his or her own thoughts to the relevant cognitive distortions from the list previously reviewed. This can then lay the groundwork for future sessions that involve coming up with a rational response directed to the particular distortion identified. Thoughts can represent more than one cognitive distortion, and it can be useful for therapists to help clients identify the most common ones that their clients tend to do.

One potential pitfall in this process can involve the therapist being too particular about the specific distortion. For example, if a client identifies his or her thought as being "all or nothing" and the more appropriate term is "fortune-telling," it would be important to simply ask why they saw it as "all or nothing" instead of necessarily spending too much time matching to the most correct specific type of cognitive distortion. Questions that elicit the reasons clients label the terms help lay the ground-work for the formulation of a rational response.

An exception to this has to do with the distortion "maladaptive think-ing." This type of thought is defined as, "You focus on a thought that may be true but over which you have no control. Excessively thinking about it can be self-critical or can distract you from an important task or from attempting new behaviors." Clients tend to label thoughts as mal-adaptive thinking when, objectively, they may not be true. For example, a thought like "I will never be happy because of all of the things I have to do to control my diabetes" or "I have HIV because I am a bad person" should not be labeled "maladaptive thinking," because this would imply that the therapist agrees with the thought. Thoughts like "I have a medi-cal illness and therefore I have limitations" may, however, be "maladap-tive thinking" if the client dwells on this excessively and allows the thoughts to keep him or her from doing things that he or she can actu-ally do.

Discuss each one and highlight the connection between thinking and mood. If time permits, you may perform this exercise with the client multiple times. Whenever possible, the client should list thoughts speci-fically related to his or her illness and self-care behaviors.

Upcoming Sessions

As previously mentioned, it will take approximately five sessions to de-liver the information in this module. The next few sessions will involve teaching the client how to identify negative automatic thinking and its impact on situations. The client will also practice the cognitive restruc-turing skills taught here.

Homework

✎ Client should continue all aspects of the program (practicing adher-ence skills from the Life-Steps module, completing the Activity Log, and engaging in pleasant alternative activities on a daily basis).

- ✎ Have client read the Preliminary Instructions for Cognitive Restructuring in the workbook to assist with identifying automatic thoughts and matching them to distortions.

- ✎ Using the Thought Record, the client should repeat the process of identifying automatic thoughts and matching them to cognitive distortions for at least two situations that are also listed on the Activity Log during the week.

- ✎ For the therapist: Discuss possible situations that the client could work on in the upcoming week.

- ✎ For the therapist: Discuss anticipated problems that may prevent the client from completing homework.

COGNITIVE RESTRUCTURING *Part II*

Materials Needed

- Cognitive Restructuring II: Formulating a Rational Response
- Thought Record

Outline

- Set agenda
- Review depression score on CES-D and discuss with client
- Review client's treatment adherence over the previous week— problem-solve any emerging difficulties or slips
- Review material and homework from previous session and modules
- Introduce and discuss rational responses

- Work with client to determine the role of core beliefs in influencing the way he or she interprets situations

- Assign homework

Set Agenda

In these remaining sessions of the cognitive restructuring module, you will explain to the client the concept of rational responses. The client will continue to work on identifying ATs and cognitive distortions for various situations.

Review of Depression Severity on CES-D

As in every session, the client completes the CES-D self-report measure of depression. Briefly review the score and take note of any symptoms that may have changed from the last measurement. Remember, as therapy progresses it can be helpful to review the total score for each of the preceding sessions in order to examine what might be helpful in treatment and what might not. Be sure to track scores using the Progress Summary Chart provided in chapter 3.

Review of Adherence and Any Medical Changes

The client also completes the Weekly Adherence Assessment Form. Be sure to assess any medical changes since the last session, including changes in symptoms or emergence of new symptoms, or new test results. Also review the relation of these medical changes to adherence behavior and correlation with mood. When reviewing the adherence form, it is important to make a plan and a backup plan for any slips in adherence from the previous week.

Review: CBT Model of Depression

Review the model with the client and remind him or her of the cognitive, behavioral, and physical components of depression and how they interact, making it easier for depression and poor adherence and poor self-care to continue. If necessary, refer back to the copy of the client's completed CBT model from chapter 3. Remind the client that this module will focus on the cognitive component of depression.

Review: Life-Steps

Remind the client how to effectively follow the medical regimen prescribed by his or her doctor or other health care provider. Review the importance of self-care behaviors and medical adherence, as well as the problem-solving technique (AIM). Make additional plans or backup plans for any new strategy that did not work out.

Review: Activity Scheduling

Spend time carefully reviewing activity scheduling, using the client's completed Activity Log for the previous week to point out times when mood was elevated and times when mood was depressed. Use this as a justification to maximize pleasurable activities. Look for any patterns with respect to symptoms (or, for diabetic patients, glucose levels) and their relationship to mood.

Review: Cognitive Restructuring: Part I

Review the rationale for cognitive restructuring and the role of the subsequent sessions in completing this module. Help with any problems the client may have with activity scheduling that cannot be solved with cognitive restructuring.

Review the client's completed Thought Records for each of the two situations for which he or she chose to record automatic thoughts and cognitive distortions. Discuss each situation individually. If the client has not completed this homework exercise, discuss the reasons why. If necessary, refer back to motivational interviewing (see Module 1) and complete the exercise during the session.

Rational Responses

Review reasons for rethinking situations that make one feel depressed or overwhelmed. Explain "coaching styles" and use the coaching metaphor provided to illustrate the importance of thinking in ways that are helpful, that make one feel better, and that are realistic.

Coaching Metaphor

This is a story about Little League baseball. I talk about Little League baseball because of the amazing parents and coaches involved. And by "amazing" I don't mean good. I mean extreme.

But this story doesn't start with the coaches or the parents. It starts with Johnny, who is a Little League player in the outfield. His job is to catch fly balls and return them to the infield players. On this particular day of our story, Johnny is in the outfield. And "crack!"—one of the players on the other team hits a fly ball. The ball is coming to Johnny. Johnny raises his glove. The ball is coming to him, it is coming to him . . . and it goes over his head. Johnny misses the ball, and the other team scores a run.

Now there are a number of ways a coach can respond to this situation. Let's take Coach A first. Coach A is the type of coach who will come out on the field and shout:

I can't believe you missed that ball! Anyone could have caught it! My dog could have caught it! You screw up like that again and you'll be sitting on the bench! That was lousy!

Coach A then storms off the field. At this point, if Johnny is anything like I am, he is standing there, tense, tight, trying not to cry, and praying that another ball is not hit to him. If a ball does come to him, Johnny will probably miss it. After all, he is tense, tight, and may see four balls coming to him because of the tears in his eyes. Also, if we are Johnny's parents, we may see more profound changes after the game: Johnny, who typically places his baseball glove on the mantle, now throws it under his bed. And before the next game, he may complain that his stomach hurts, that perhaps he should not go to the game. This is the scenario with Coach A.

Now let's go back to the original event and play it differently. Johnny has just missed the fly ball, and now Coach B comes out on the field. Coach B says:

> *Well, you missed that one. Here is what I want you to remember: fly balls always look like they are farther away than they really are. Also, it is much easier to run forward than to back up. Because of this, I want you to prepare for the ball by taking a few extra steps backward. Run forward if you need to, but try to catch it at chest level, so you can adjust your hand if you misjudge the ball. Let's see how you do next time.*

Coach B leaves the field. How does Johnny feel? Well, he is not happy. After all, he missed the ball—but there are a number of important differences from the way he felt with Coach A. He is not as tense or tight, and if a fly ball does come to him, he knows what to do differently to catch it. And because he does not have tears in his eyes, he may actually see the ball accurately. He may catch the next one.

So, if we were the type of parent who eventually wants Johnny to make the major leagues, we would pick Coach B, because he teaches Johnny how to be a more effective player. Johnny knows what to do differently, may catch more balls, and may excel at the game. But if we don't care whether Johnny makes the major leagues—because baseball is a game and one is supposed to be able to enjoy a game—then we would still pick Coach B. We pick Coach B because we care whether Johnny enjoys the game. With Coach B, Johnny knows what to do differently; he is not tight, tense, and ready to cry; he may catch a few balls; and he may enjoy the game. And he may continue to place his glove on the mantel.

Now, while we may all select Coach B for Johnny, we rarely choose the view of Coach B for the way we talk to ourselves. Think about your last mistake. Did you say, "I can't believe I did that! I am so stupid! What a jerk!" These are Coach A thoughts, and they have approximately the same effect on us that they do on Johnny. They make us feel tense and tight, and sometimes make us feel like crying. And this style of coaching rarely makes us do better in the future. If you are only concerned about productivity (making the major leagues), you would pick Coach B. And if you were concerned with enjoying life, while guiding yourself effectively for both joy and productivity, you would still pick Coach B.

Keep in mind that we are not talking about how we coach ourselves in a baseball game. We are talking about how we coach ourselves in life, and our enjoyment of life.

During the next week, I would like you to listen to see how you are coaching yourself. And if you hear Coach A, remember this story and see if you can replace Coach A with Coach B. (Adapted from Otto, 1999)

Forming Rational Responses

Use the Cognitive Restructuring II: Formulating a Rational Response information sheet provided as a guide for this explanation. The client can follow along using the copy in the workbook.

Cognitive Restructuring II: Formulating a Rational Response

The purpose of cognitive restructuring is to help promote optimal thinking when you are depressed or feeling medically sick. Throughout the week, when you are feeling sad or overwhelmed or upset about your illness, continue to list your thoughts for each situation on the Thought Record in your workbook. If you are anticipating a stressful situation or a task that is making you feel overwhelmed, write out your thoughts regarding this situation. If a situation has already passed, and you find that you are thinking about it negatively, list your thoughts for this situation.

*The **first column** of the Thought Record is for you to provide a description of the situation.*

*The **second column** is for you to list your thoughts during a stressful, overwhelming, or uncontrollable situation.*

*The **third column** is for you to write down what emotions you are having and what your mood is like when thinking these thoughts (e.g., depressed, sad, angry).*

*The **fourth column** is for you to see whether your thoughts match the list of "cognitive distortions." These may include:*

All-or-nothing thinking	*Emotional reasoning*
Overgeneralizations	*"Should" statements*
Jumping to conclusions:	*Labeling and mislabeling*
Fortune-telling/mind reading	*Personalization*
Magnification/minimization	*Maladaptive thinking*

*In the **fifth column**, try to come up with a rational response to each thought or to the most important negative thought. The rational response is a statement that you can say to yourself to try to feel better about the situation. Questions to help come up with this rational response can include:*

What is the evidence that this thought is true?

Is there an alternate explanation?

What is the worst thing that can happen?

Has this situation unreasonably grown in importance?

What would a good coach say about this situation?

Have I done what I can do to control it?

If I were to do anything else, would this help or hinder the situation?

Am I worrying excessively about this?

What would a good friend say to me about this situation?

What would I say to a good friend about this situation if he/she were going through it?

Why is this statement a cognitive distortion?

Using the client's completed Thought Records from last week, help him or her to formulate rational responses to each of the automatic thoughts listed. An example of a completed Thought Record with rational responses is shown in figure 6.2.

The client should ask the following questions:

- What is the evidence that this thought is true?

- Is there an alternate explanation?

- What is the worst thing that can happen?

- Has this situation unreasonably grown in importance?

- What would a good coach say about this situation?

- Have I done what I can do to control it?

- If I were to do anything else, would this help or hinder the situation?

- Am I worrying excessively about this?

- What would a good friend say to me about this situation?

- What would I say to a good friend about this situation if he/she were going through it?

- Why is this statement a cognitive distortion?

Testing Automatic Thoughts in Real-Life Situations

When possible, clients can be assigned to test negative thoughts through experience. This will be done in conjunction with the activity scheduling in which the client is hopefully now engaging. Regarding upcoming activities, the client can use the Thought Record to help prepare for an

Thought Record

Time and situation	Automatic thoughts (what was going through your head?)	Mood and intensity of mood (0–100)	Cognitive distortions (match thoughts from list)	Rational response
Tues. afternoon: Went to cookout with my girlfriend and daughter.	Good memories (at first) of wife who passed away.	First, felt really good (80)		I can only do my best in terms of taking care of myself.
	I don't take care of myself well enough.	A little sad (60)	"Should" thinking	Although I have an illness, there are things I can do to take good care of myself and can therefore live a longer life.
	Because of this, I won't live long enough to have these kinds of outings with my family.	Very sad and guilty (95)	Fortune-telling "Should" thinking	
	My daughter lost her mother and has a horrible father.		Labeling	I do the best I can to take care of my daughter.
Weds. morning: I woke up and knew it was time to take my medications but I had to push myself to get out of bed and so I just didn't take them.	I'm never going to be healthy. I can't take care of myself. I am a horrible person.	Disappointed in myself (80) Hopeless (95)	Catastrophizing Labeling	I have been better at taking my meds. Today was a slip. Missing meds one morning does not mean I am a horrible person.

Figure 6.2.

Example of Completed Thought Record

upcoming situation. The client can prepare in advance and set realistic goals. After the situation, the client is encouraged to look back at the Thought Record completed before entering into the situation to determine how accurate his or her automatic thoughts and rational responses were.

Core Beliefs

As the treatment continues, the therapist may begin to notice patterns in the client's automatic thoughts. By asking questions for the thoughts, such as "Why would this be bad?" or "What makes that upsetting?" the therapist and the client can collaboratively determine the role of core beliefs in "coloring" the client's interpretation of the situations.

This is known as the "downward spiral" technique (A. Beck, 1987; J. S. Beck, 1995). As sessions continue, the therapist should revise the initial model of cognitive, behavioral, and physiological components but include the underlying "core beliefs" as a deeper aspect of the cognitive component of depression that lies below any surface thoughts. Examples of core beliefs include "Because of my illness, I am worthless" and "I am unlovable."

The concept of core beliefs is familiar to trained cognitive-behavioral therapists and is a standard component of CBT for depression (see also Persons, 1989). It is particularly relevant for clients who have "treatment resistance," or more chronic depression. Therapists who need more information about the techniques used to elicit and restructure core beliefs should consult more detailed treatments of the practice of CBT (e.g., J. S. Beck, 1995).

Homework

✎ The client should continue all aspects of the program (practicing adherence skills from the Life-Steps module, completing the Activity Log, and engaging in pleasant alternative activities on a daily basis).

✎ Instruct the client to list automatic thoughts, cognitive distortions, and rational responses on the Thought Record over the course of the following week.

✎ For the therapist: Discuss possible situations that the client could work on in the upcoming week.

✎ For the therapist: Discuss anticipated problems that may prevent the client from completing homework.

Chapter 7   *Module 5: Problem Solving*

(Corresponds to chapter 7 of the workbook)

Materials Needed

- Problem-Solving Sheet
- Note cards or plain paper

Outline

- Set agenda
- Review depression score on CES-D and discuss with client
- Review client's treatment adherence over the previous week and problem-solve any emerging difficulties or slips
- Review material and homework from previous modules
- Teach client five steps of problem solving
- Teach client the method of breaking seemingly overwhelming problems into small, manageable steps
- Use examples to illustrate the process of problem solving
- Assign homework

Set Agenda

Over the course of the next two sessions you will teach the client problem-solving skills. Problem-solving training (D'Zurilla, 1986) will involve teaching clients how to take an overwhelming task and break it into manageable steps, with the goal of reducing cognitive avoidance. Additional problem-solving techniques involve training in articulation of the problem, coming up with possible solutions, and selecting the best possible solution. This approach is used for depression (Nezu & Perri, 1989) and has specific application to coping with chronic illness (Nezu, Nezu, Friedman, Faddis, & Houts, 1998). We have adapted these techniques for use in this program.

Review of Depression Severity on CES-D

As in every session, the client completes the CES-D self-report measure of depression. Briefly review the score and take note of any symptoms that may have changed from the last measurement. Remember, as therapy progresses it can be helpful to review the total score for each of the preceding sessions in order to examine what might be helpful in treatment and what might not. Be sure to track scores using the Progress Summary Chart provided in chapter 3.

Review of Adherence and Any Medical Changes

The client also completes the Weekly Adherence Assessment Form. This form is included in the corresponding client workbook. Be sure to assess any medical changes since the last session, including changes in symptoms or emergence of new symptoms, or new test results. Also review the relation of these medical changes to adherence behavior and correlation with mood.

Review of Previous Modules and Homework

Review: CBT Model of Depression

Review the model with the client and remind him or her of the cognitive, behavioral, and physical components of depression and how they interact, making it easier for depression and poor adherence and poor self-care to continue. If necessary, refer back to the copy of the client's completed CBT model from chapter 3. Point out that the problem-solving module attacks both the cognitive and the behavioral components of depression. The reason is that we seek to help people feel better about what they have to do by making the tasks easier. Hence the goals get done, and the behavioral component is affected.

Review: Life-Steps

Remind the client how to effectively follow the medical regimen prescribed by his or her doctor or other health care provider. Review the importance of self-care behaviors and medical adherence, as well as the problem-solving technique (AIM). Make additional plans or backup plans for any new strategy that did not work out.

Review: Activity Scheduling

Spend time carefully reviewing activity scheduling, using the client's completed Activity Log for the previous week to point out times when his or her mood was elevated and times when his or her mood was depressed. Use this as a justification to maximize pleasurable activities. Look for any patterns with respect to symptoms (or, for diabetic patients, glucose levels) and their relationship to mood. The client should continue to monitor his or her daily activities and mood using the Activity Log from the workbook. Continue to make sure that the client is maximizing the times that he or she can engage in positive events.

Review: Cognitive Restructuring

Discuss any questions the client may have regarding cognitive restructuring. Review how thoughts and beliefs can impact the client's view of certain situations. Be sure the client is continuing to use cognitive restructuring in situations that make him or her upset. Review any upsetting events over the previous week and discuss them in terms of whether the client used cognitive restructuring to think more adaptively about them.

Problem Solving

Provide the client with the following rationale for problem solving:

When people are depressed, many tasks seem overwhelming. It is difficult to get started. This can become more difficult when one also is coping with a medical illness and needs to take care of complicated self-care issues while also coping with depression.

Additionally, when people are depressed, it can be difficult to pick an action plan. When living with chronic illness, multiple stressors can exist, and no solution may be ideal—however, inaction can make the situation worse.

Problem solving will help with these issues.

Problem-Solving Training

Explain to the client that problem solving involves two skills. First is the ability to select a plan of action, even if there is no ideal solution available. Second is the ability to take an overwhelming task and break it down into manageable steps. The aim of this session is to teach the client how to effectively use the technique of problem solving in his or her own life.

Five Steps of Problem Solving

Use these instructions in conjunction with the sample Problem-Solving Sheets shown in figures 7.1 and 7.2. You may photocopy these samples and distribute them to the client or download copies from the Treatments *ThatWork*™ website at http://www.oup.com/us/ttw.

Problem-Solving Sheet

Statement of the problem: <u>I do not exercise enough but would like to because it will help improve</u> <u>my health.</u>

Instructions:

1) List all of the possible solutions that you can think of. List them even if you think they don't make sense, or you don't think you would do them. The point is to come up with *as many solutions as possible.*
2) List the pros and cons of each solution.
3) After listing the pros and cons of each, review the whole list, and give a rating to each solution.
4) Use additional copies of this sheet as needed (even if it's for the same problem).

Possible Solution	Pros of Solution	Cons of Solution	Overall Rating of Solution (1–10)
Walk to work instead of drive	I will get fresh air, get energized, and have a clearer head. Less stress that comes with driving.	I may get a little sweaty. I would need to carry a change of clothes. Wake up earlier to allow for more commute time.	7
Take the stairs instead of elevator	Takes little time. I don't have to leave home/work.	My legs get sore after. I feel lazy sometimes because it's not easy.	6
Join a gym	Variety: Do a cardio class. Starting lifting weights. Meet people.	It costs money. I would need to make time to go.	8
Take a yoga class	Improve flexibility. Decrease stress. Be with other people.	I may get embarrassed since I've never done it before and am not flexible. It costs money.	7

Figure 7.1

Example of Completed Problem-Solving Sheet

Problem-Solving Sheet

Statement of the problem: _I never get the information I need from my doctor._

Instructions:

1) List all of the possible solutions that you can think of. List them even if you think they don't make sense, or you don't think you would do them. The point is to come up with *as many solutions as possible.*
2) List the pros and cons of each solution.
3) After listing the pros and cons of each, review the whole list, and give a rating to each solution.
4) Use additional copies of this sheet as needed (even if it's for the same problem).

Possible Solution	Pros of Solution	Cons of Solution	Overall Rating of Solution (1–10)
Have someone come with me.	That person could help listen to the answers and then remind me.	I don't know who to ask, everyone is busy during the day.	5
Try to remember to ask the questions.	Hopefully it would work.	This is what I do now, and I don't seem to be getting my questions answered.	2
Make a list of what I want to ask her about.	I would get my questions answered.	I would feel stupid with a list. I would have to put in time to make the list.	6
Change doctors.	Could see if someone else is better at explaining things. Maybe a new one would have more time.	Most doctors don't have time. I get along with this doctor.	5
Tell the doctor that I have a hard time remembering what she says and getting my questions asked.	The doctor would possibly make a better effort to make sure that I understand. I would feel more comfortable asking questions.	I would feel awkward having this type of conversation.	6

Figure 7.2.

Example of Completed Problem-Solving Sheet

Step 1. Articulate the Problem

Try to get the client to describe the problem in as few words as possible—one or two sentences at most. Examples include:

- I can't decide whether I should switch my health care provider.

- I can't decide what to do about my housing situation.

- I am in debt due to medical expenses.

Step 2. List All Possible Solutions

In the first column of the Problem-Solving Sheet, the client should try to come up with a number of solutions—regardless of how possible they are, what the consequences may be, or whether they are silly or outrageous. The idea is to generate a list of as many solutions as possible. Notably, we find that listing the solutions can be a difficult task for clients who feel that they are in a "rut." Hence, we encourage creativity with this—trying to find solutions that they may not have thought of, or specifically articulate solutions that may seem obvious.

Step 3. List the Pros and Cons of Each Solution

Now is the time for the client to realistically appraise each solution. In the Pros and Cons columns of the sheet, the client should figure out what he or she really thinks would happen if he or she selected that solution. The advantages (pros) and disadvantages (cons) of each should be listed.

Step 4. Rate Each Solution

Using the final column, the client should rate the solution on a scale from 1–10. This should be done as objectively as possible.

Step 5. Implement the Best Option

Now that the client has rated each possible solution on a scale of 1–10, review each option and its rating. Look at the one that is rated the highest. Determine whether this is really the solution that the client would like to pick. The next part of problem solving involves trying to break the solution down into manageable steps. Use of cognitive restructuring can also be applied here if there are negative thoughts related to inaction or if there are excessively negative projections about the potential outcome of the situations.

Use the sample completed Problem-Solving Sheets to show the client examples of how to select action plans for particular problems.

Steps for Breaking Large Tasks Into Manageable Steps

1. Choose a problem that exists for your client on which he or she is avoiding action. Ideally, this can be the problem just discussed in the previous skill on selecting an action plan.

   List the steps that must be completed. This can be done using small note cards or plain paper. Ask questions such as, *"What is the first thing that you would need to do to make this happen? What is next?"*

2. For each step, make sure that it is manageable.

   Have the client ask him- or herself, "Is this something that I could realistically complete in one day?" and "Is this something that I would want to put off doing?"

   If any step seems too overwhelming, break that step down into further manageable steps.

One of the potential pitfalls here is that clients will not want to implement any of the solutions because they fear the consequences or feel that they cannot do them. This is where it is important to use cognitive restructuring as needed if completing any of the tasks would cause the client to experience anxiety or depressed mood. Going back and forth between the problem-solving module and the cognitive restructuring module can be an integral part of progress here.

Homework

✎ Client should continue all aspects of the program (practicing adherence skills from the Life-Steps module, completing the Activity Log, engaging in pleasant alternative activities on a daily basis, and using cognitive restructuring methods as needed).

✎ Instruct client to use the formal problem-solving method when necessary and record possible solutions on the Problem-Solving Sheet.

Chapter 8

Module 6: Relaxation Training and Diaphragmatic Breathing

(Corresponds to chapter 8 of the workbook)

Outline

- Set agenda

- Review depression score on CES-D and discuss with client

- Review client's treatment adherence over the previous week and problem-solve any emerging difficulties or slips

- Review material and homework from previous modules

- Teach breathing retraining and progressive muscle relaxation

- Assign homework

Set Agenda

In this module, the focus is on teaching the client how to relax in situations that may cause stress or pain. This skill can be adapted for use in managing side effects of medications, to help in preparation for any painful medical procedures, and to help with sleep.

Progressive muscle relaxation and breathing retraining are key components to anxiety management and stress reduction programs. They are also widely used in behavioral medicine approaches to coping with body pain, headache, and nausea (Cotanch, 1983; Smith, 1987; Turner & Chapman, 1982).

Training in diaphragmatic breathing helps clients to ground themselves and relax during times of stress and to directly cope with symptoms.

With the help of the therapist, the participant will make a relaxation tape, which will involve training in cue-controlled relaxation.

Review of Depression Severity on CES-D

As in every session, the client completes the CES-D self-report measure of depression. Briefly review the score and take note of any symptoms that may have changed from the last measurement. Remember, as therapy progresses it can be helpful to review the total score for each of the preceding sessions in order to examine what might be helpful in treatment and what might not. Be sure to track scores using the Progress Summary Chart provided in chapter 3.

Review of Adherence and Any Medical Changes

The client also completes the Weekly Adherence Assessment Form. Be sure to assess any medical changes since the last session, including changes in symptoms or emergence of new symptoms, or new test results. Also review the relation of these medical changes to adherence behavior and correlation with mood.

Review of Previous Modules

Review: CBT Model of Depression

Review the model with the client and remind him or her of the cognitive, behavioral, and physical components of depression and how they interact, making it easier for depression and poor adherence or poor self-care to continue. If necessary, refer back to the copy of the client's completed CBT model from chapter 3.

Review: Life-Steps

Remind client how to effectively follow the medical regimen prescribed by his or her doctor or other health care provider. Review the importance of self-care behaviors and medical adherence, as well as the problem-solving technique (AIM). Make additional plans or backup plans for any new strategy that did not work out.

Review: Activity Scheduling

Spend time carefully reviewing activity scheduling, using the client's completed Activity Log for the previous week to point out times when his or her mood was elevated and times when his or her mood was depressed. Use this as a justification to maximize pleasurable activities. Look for any patterns with respect to symptoms (or, for diabetic patients, glucose levels) and their relationship to mood. The client should continue to monitor daily activities and mood using the Activity Log from the workbook.

Review: Cognitive Restructuring

Discuss any questions the client may have regarding cognitive restructuring. Review how thoughts and beliefs can impact the client's view of certain situations. Be sure the client is continuing to use cognitive restructuring in situations that make him or her upset. Review any upsetting events over the previous week and discuss them in terms of whether the client used the cognitive restructuring to think more adaptively about them.

Review: Problem Solving

Discuss the extent to which problems have been broken down into steps. Review any completed problem-solving worksheets and encourage the client to continue to use these skills. Review any areas in which the skills are not understood or being utilized and attempt to clarify any remaining questions.

Breathing Retraining

The object of breathing retraining is to teach the client to use calm, slow breathing in order to achieve a relaxed state. Overbreathing and chest breathing, which many people tend to do when feeling anxious, can actually exacerbate anxiety symptoms. Instead, it is more effective to breathe from the diaphragm. Chest breathing involves filling your lungs with air, forcing the chest upward and outward to expand, so that you are taking relatively shallow breaths. Diaphragmatic breathing, on the other hand, keeps your chest relaxed and lets the diaphragm, the smooth muscle at the bottom of the lungs, do all the work. When you inhale, the diaphragm moves down, creating a vacuum and pulling air in. This technique results in deeper breaths, which is a healthier and fuller way to take in oxygen.

Diaphragmatic Breathing Technique

Have the client practice diaphragmatic breathing during the session. Instruct the client to place one hand on the stomach and the other on the chest. Teach the client to differentiate between chest breathing and diaphragmatic breathing by having him or her inhale slowly and watch which hand moves. Chest breathing occurs when the hand on the chest moves; diaphragmatic breathing is occurring when the hand on the stomach moves.

You may use the following sample dialogue to guide the client through the process of diaphragmatic breathing:

Get into a comfortable position. Now, slowly inhale through your nose. As you inhale, count slowly to three and feel your stomach expand with your hand. Hold the breath for one second and then slowly exhale while also counting to three. When you inhale, think of the word "inhale." When you exhale, think of the word "relax."

Have the client repeat this exercise until he or she is able to do it correctly. Like any skill, it takes practice to master.

Progressive Muscle Relaxation

Just like diaphragmatic breathing, muscle relaxation is a skill that can be learned as long as it is practiced regularly. It helps with tension, with certain side effects caused by medication, and with pain and stress.

You may use the following sample dialogue to introduce progressive muscle relaxation to the client:

We will do a procedure called progressive muscle relaxation. It involves tensing, then relaxing, various muscle groups, one at a time. It takes about 25 minutes, and by the time you are done, your whole body is relaxed.

Once you are relaxed, the trick is to make a mental note of what the relaxation feels like. You can then apply this to situations of stress, in conjunction with slow breathing, when doing the whole procedure is not possible. We will make a tape of the progressive muscle relaxation procedure, so that you can take it home and practice.

Ask the client if he or she has any questions or concerns before continuing. Use a blank cassette tape (or digital audio recorder) to record the relaxation procedure.

Therapist Note: There are some relaxation "tapes" available as MP3 files that can be found on public access Internet sites. Therapists may wish to locate some this way, listen to them, and give them to clients.

You may use the following script to facilitate the relaxation exercise.

Progressive Muscle Relaxation Script

The following outline can be used to create a tape recording of the progressive muscle relaxation procedure. Use a slow, relaxing, somewhat monotonous tone. Progressive muscle relaxation involves tensing, then relaxing all of the different muscle groups. Muscles should be tensed for approximately 5 seconds each, and then relaxed for at least 10 seconds. Clients should be instructed to relax or "let go" all at once, so that the contrast between tension and relaxation can be achieved. Before starting the procedure, go over what it will look like to tense each muscle group. Use the list of muscle groups provided.

Start recording and use the following sample dialogue:

> *Sit comfortably in the chair and relax as much as possible. Breathe calmly and regularly with your stomach.* (Wait a few seconds.) *Pay attention to my voice. If, as we go through this, your mind starts to wander, just bring your attention back to the relaxation procedure.*

You may use the following sample dialogue for each muscle group.

> *At this point, I want you to tense your _____. Hold it . . . now relax . . . relax the muscles in your _____ . . . notice the difference between the tension and the relaxation.*
>
> 1. *Tense the hands and forearms by making fists and holding them (each hand separately).*
> 2. *Tense the biceps by bending your elbows and bringing your hands to your shoulders (each separately).*
> 3. *Tense your shoulders by bringing them up to your ears (both together).*
> 4. *Tense your upper face by raising your eyebrows while keeping your eyes closed.*
> 5. *Tense your lower face by clenching your teeth, tensing your jaws, and pressing your lips together while frowning.*
> 6. *Tense your chest by taking a deep chest breath and holding it.*
> 7. *Tense your stomach by pushing your stomach out.*
> 8. *Tense your back by bending your back in a curve.*
> 9. *Tense your thighs by pressing your heels to the floor.*
> 10. *Tense your calves by pressing your feet and toes down.*
> 11. *Tense your feet by bending your feet up toward your face and scrunching your toes.*

After you go through the entire procedure of systematically tensing and releasing/relaxing each muscle group, continue with the following.

> *Now you can get even more relaxed by continuing to breathe and relax. Your entire body is relaxed. Continue breathing and relaxing,*

calmly and regularly, to achieve an even deeper level of relaxation. (Wait a full minute.)

Now what I want to do is help you become even more relaxed. I am going to slowly count from 20 to 1. Each time I get to another number, I want you to get even more relaxed. Even though it might seem that you are fully relaxed, try to go that extra bit (count slowly . . . 20 to 1).

At this point I want you to make a mental note of your degree of relaxation right now. Notice what it feels like to be relaxed. There is no tension in your body and you are totally relaxed. Remember what this feels like. I am going to let you breathe and relax for another minute. As you breathe, think of the word inhale every time you inhale, and think of the word relax every time you exhale. If your mind starts to wander, just go back to thinking "inhale" and "relax."

(Wait another two minutes.)

We are now done with the progressive muscle relaxation training. When you are ready, you can take some time and open your eyes. (Adapted from Ost, n.d., and Otto, Jones, Craske, & Barlow, 1996)

Once again, stress to the client that muscle relaxation is a learned skill. Practice is necessary so the client can master the technique and apply it in real-life situations. Refer to the point in the script where you ask the client to make a mental note of how relaxed he or she is at that point. The idea is for the client to practice enough so that eventually he or she will be able to simply take a slow, deep breath and recover that relaxed feeling.

Homework

✎ The client should continue all aspects of the program (practicing adherence skills from the Life-Steps module, completing the Activity Log, engaging in pleasant alternative activities on a daily basis, and using cognitive restructuring and problem-solving methods as needed).

✎ Instruct the client to practice diaphragmatic breathing twice per day (once in the morning and once in the evening).

✎ Have the client practice relaxation training as much as possible. Once per day is ideal, but at least three to four times per week is acceptable.

✎ The client should record breathing exercise and relaxation training on the Breathing Retraining and Progressive Muscle Relaxation: Practice Log in the workbook.

Chapter 9 *Module 7: Review, Maintenance, and Relapse Prevention*

(Corresponds to chapter 9 of the workbook)

Outline

- Set agenda

- Review depression score on CES-D and discuss with client

- Review client's treatment adherence over the previous week

- Review progress and usefulness of treatment strategies

- Review homework

- Discuss transition to becoming one's own therapist

- Discuss maintenance of gains

- Discuss troubleshooting and address relapse prevention

- Assign continued "homework"

Set Agenda

This module is a review of all treatment strategies learned in previous sessions. It also addresses ways to maintain changes to help clients transition to becoming their own therapists.

Review of Depression Severity on CES-D

As done in the beginning of all sessions, the client completes the CES-D self-report measure of depression. Briefly review the score and take note of any symptoms that may have changed from the last measurement.

Review the total score for each of the preceding sessions and examine what may have been helpful in treatment and what may not have been helpful for the client. Be sure to track scores using the Progress Summary Chart. As in the previous sessions, this may also be a discussion point regarding therapy "homework"—that is, if a client completes the "homework" and feels better, this point can be emphasized. If the client has not engaged in behavioral change and his or her symptoms of depression have not changed, this fact could be utilized to increase motivation in future sessions.

Review of Adherence and Any Medical Changes

The client also completes the Weekly Adherence Assessment Form. Assess any medical changes since the last session, including changes in symptoms or emergence of new symptoms, or new test results. Also review the correlation of these medical changes with both adherence behavior and mood. Identify triggers for missed doses, such as running out of medication or thoughts about not wanting or needing to take medication. Problem-solve as necessary to continue to improve adherence and maintain improvements.

Review of Last Session

Remind client that the last session focused on using relaxation skills to help ground him- or herself, to relax in the face of stress, and to directly cope with any symptoms. Review the use of diaphragmatic breathing and progressive muscle relaxation skills. Refer back to the copy of the client's CBT model completed during the psychoeducation module and discuss the relation of use of relaxation skills to physical health, adherence behavior, and overall mood.

Review of Previous Modules and Homework

Review skills learned in each previous session and discuss their role in helping to interrupt the cycle of depression and improving adherence.

Review: CBT Model of Depression

Review the model with the client and remind him or her of the cognitive, behavioral, and physical components of depression and how they interact, making it easier for depression and poor adherence and poor self-care to continue. If necessary, refer back to the copy of the client's completed CBT model from chapter 3.

Review: Life-Steps

Review skills learned during the Life-Steps module that help the client follow the medical regimen prescribed by his or her health care provider. Review the importance of self-care behaviors and medical adherence, as well as the problem-solving technique (AIM), in relation to continuing to maintain improvements in symptoms and depression.

Review: Activity Scheduling

Review any patterns of engaging in pleasurable activities and self-care behaviors with respect to medical symptoms and their relationship to mood.

Review: Cognitive Restructuring

Discuss any questions the client may have regarding cognitive restructuring. Review how thoughts and core beliefs can impact the client's view of him- or herself, others, and various situations. Discuss how negative thoughts can affect use of skills to improve adherence and mood.

Review: Problem Solving

Review problem solving and use of skills to select a plan of action and to take an overwhelming task and break it down into manageable steps.

Discuss Transition to Becoming One's Own Therapist

The key to a successful transition to becoming one's own therapist is persistent use of the skills learned in this program and gaining mastery over them. Overemphasize this point with the client by suggesting that *these strategies and skills need to be practiced regularly so that they become more automatic and habitual.* In this way, when regular sessions of treatment end, the client's own program of treatment begins, and he or she can work to solidify and expand the skills and strategies learned.

Client Progress

In order to help the client transition to this next phase of treatment in which he or she takes over the role as the therapist, it is important for the client to recognize the nature of any benefits achieved. One way to look at progress is to use the Progress Summary Chart and review treatment adherence, depression, and homework ratings over treatment sessions. If there are sudden gains in treatment—dramatic or significant reductions in a depression score or increased adherence in a given week—it is important to discuss what occurred that week that caused the change (i.e., the client finally set up a mail-in prescription to avoid running out of medications, started exercising two times per week, etc.)

Usefulness of Treatment Strategies

In addition to attempting to recall which sessions produced the most gains, review the treatment strategies and determine how useful they have been for the client. Complete the Treatment Strategies and Usefulness Chart with the client and discuss it in session. This chart is also included in the client workbook.

As the discussion progresses, provide positive feedback regarding the approaches that worked and emphasize the importance of continuing to use them. If there are strategies that have not worked, these do not need to be continued. However, try to also problem-solve any difficul-

Table 9.1. Treatment Strategies and Usefulness Chart

Instructions: Please rate the usefulness of each strategy to you, from 0 to 100 (0 = Didn't help at all; 100 = Was extremely important for me). Also, take some time to provide notes to yourself about why you think each strategy worked or didn't work to help you, and figure out which strategies might be most helpful for you to practice over the next month.

Treatment Strategies	Usefulness Ratings	Notes About Your Application/ Usefulness of Strategies
Psychoeducation		
Understanding the relationship between thoughts, behaviors, and physical symptoms and depression and adherence Motivational exercise: weighing pros and cons of changing vs. not changing		
Adherence Training (Life-Steps)		
Understanding the importance of treatment adherence Plan for transportation to medical appointments Plan for obtaining medications or other self-care items Plan for optimizing communication with medical and mental health care providers Plan for coping with side effects of medications and medical regimen Formulate a daily schedule for medications and other self-care behaviors Plan for storing medications Develop cues for taking medications or implementing other self-care procedures Prepare for adaptively coping with slips in adherence and preventing relapse		
Activity Scheduling		
Understand the relationship between activities and mood Incorporate activities that involve pleasure or mastery into daily schedule		

continued

Table 9.1. Treatment Strategies and Usefulness Chart *continued*

Treatment Strategies	Usefulness Ratings	Notes About Your Application/ Usefulness of Strategies
Cognitive Restructuring (Adaptive Thinking) Identify automatic thoughts Identify cognitive distortions Rethink situations that make you feel bad and develop rational response to automatic thought Test automatic thoughts in real-life situations (like during a new activity) Use downward spiral technique and identify core beliefs		
Problem Solving Articulate the problem Articulate possible solutions Select the best possible solution Set a plan of action to implement the solution Break tasks into manageable steps		
Relaxation Training Diaphragmatic breathing Progressive muscle relaxation		

ties that the client may be having with using the strategies that did not seem to work.

For example, if the client was having difficulty incorporating cardiovascular exercises into his or her weekly routine, you can say:

> *It seems like using activity scheduling to build in an exercise regimen did not work for you. It may help for us to review what your exercise goals and plan were to see if we can problem-solve some of the things that got in the way.*

What were your exercise goals? What was your exercise plan? Do you know what got in the way? When you did exercise, how did you feel right afterward? How about the following day(s)? How did you expect to feel? What did you expect to gain?

If the client's goals or plan can be improved, help the client to renegotiate them. If that activity does not seem to work for the client at all, identify new activities instead.

Maintaining Gains, Preventing Relapse, and Ending Treatment

Maintaining Gains

An important distinction for clients to be aware of is the difference between a "setback" and a "relapse." Review the Improvement Graph from chapter 4 (figure 4.4) to help the client improve his or her expectations about what behavioral change really looks like. Point to the graph and explain that most clients expect change to happen steadily and consistently and to be able to easily maintain the changes they have made. In contrast, progress usually happens with ebbs and flows over the sessions and with some dips after treatment. Explain that "setbacks" are part of progress. You may use the following sample dialogue:

Successfully completing treatment does not mean that you will not have future difficulties with symptoms. For most conditions, symptoms and the changes you have made can wax and wane over time. The key to maintaining treatment gains over the long run is to be ready for periods of increased difficulties. These periods are not signs that the treatment has failed. Instead, these periods are signals that you need to apply the skills and practice them often.

Encourage the client to use the One-Month Review Sheet provided in the workbook to refresh skills as needed. Explain that the purpose of the worksheet is to remind the client of the importance of practicing skills and to help the client think through which strategies might be important to practice. You may use the following sample dialogue to facilitate this discussion:

> *Completing the review sheet may help you to prepare to recover from missing doses (or lapsing from an exercise routine, or breaking your diet regimen), which, in the long run, is likely to occur. If a lapse occurs, the best choice is to return to your adherence program as soon as possible instead of acting on hopeless thoughts and giving up. If you can identify what led to the lapse, the information can help to solidify the skills and avoid future lapses. Lapses are normal and not a big problem. They only become a big problem when they lead to relapse and giving up on the self-care regimen.*

Troubleshooting Difficulties

It may also be helpful to match some of the symptoms the client is experiencing with some of the specific strategies used in treatment. You can use the CBT model of depression worksheet to help the client to identify his or her specific cognitions, behaviors, and physiological symptoms that the client reports experiencing when depressed.

Use table 9.2 to help the client match specific symptoms with skills that were taught in the treatment sessions.

In addition, encourage the client to use the problem-solving worksheets to more carefully consider any difficulties with symptoms. Also suggest that the client enlist the help of family and friends and/or schedule a booster session with you if these strategies are not effective in improving his or her depression or adherence.

Termination

As with any therapy, spend some time processing termination with the client. Share your thoughts about how it was for you to work with the client, noting aspects of the treatment that were especially enjoyable for you (i.e., "I know you really had doubts about being able to monitor your glucose regularly, and it was a pleasure for me to watch you work

Table 9.2 Symptoms and Skills Chart

Symptoms of Depression	Skills to Consider
I haven't been taking my medications lately because they make me feel sick.	Review Life-Steps Skills • Life-Step 2: Communicating with treatment team • Life-Step 3: Coping with side effects
I've been spending more time alone and haven't felt like doing much lately.	Monitor activities and mood on a daily basis using Activity Log Incorporate activities that involve pleasure or mastery into daily schedule
I don't feel like going out to dinner with friends and family because I need to watch my diet and don't want to have to explain my illness to them.	Identify automatic thoughts Identify cognitive distortions Record automatic thoughts and match to distortions using Thought Record Challenge automatic thoughts and come up with a rational response
I need to lose weight but I just don't know where to start.	Practice problem-solving strategies (articulate the problem, generate possible solutions, choose the best alternative) Break tasks down into manageable steps
I get so anxious and stressed out sometimes at work and I have trouble calming down.	Diaphragmatic breathing Progressive muscle relaxation

through that and get to the point now where you can't imagine not doing routine glucose checking"). Congratulate the client for all of the hard work that was put into completing this treatment program. It was demanding! However, we truly believe these skills can make a profound difference and help improve depression and adherence. Remind the client one final time to "practice, practice, practice the skills that were learned! Improvements will not magically maintain themselves. Only through continued use will they become automatic."

References

Note: The intervention approach is based on several treatment manuals for depression and related problems. Works used as resources to inform this treatment include:

Agency for Health Care Policy and Research Depression Guideline Panel. (1993a). *Depression in primary care: Vol. 1. Detection and diagnosis* (Clinical Practice Guideline No. 5; ACHPR Publication No. 93–0550). Rockville, MD: U.S. Department of Health and Human Services, Public Health Service.

Agency for Health Care Policy and Research Depression Guideline Panel. (1993b). *Depression in primary care: Vol. 2. Treatment of major depression* (Clinical Practice Guideline No. 5; ACHPR Publication No. 93–0551). Rockville, MD: U.S. Department of Health and Human Services, Public Health Service. .

Alter, M. J., Kruszon-Moran, D., Nainan, O. V., McQuillan, G. M., Gao, F., Moyer, L. A., et al. (1999). The prevalence of Hepatitis C virus infection in the United States, 1988 through 1994. *New England Journal of Medicine, 341,* 556–562.

American Cancer Society. (2006). Retrieved from http://www.cancer.org/docroot/MBC/content/MBC_4_1X_Cancer_and_Depression.asp?sitearea=MBC

American Heart Association. (2007). *Heart disease and stroke statistics—2007 update.* Dallas, TX: American Heart Association.

American Psychiatric Association. (2000). *Diagnostic and statistical manual of mental disorders* (4th ed., text rev.). Washington, DC: Author.

Ammassari, A., Murri, R., Pezzotti, P., Trotta, M. P., Ravasio, L., De Longis, P., et al. (2001). Self-reported symptoms and medication side effects influence adherence to highly active antiretroviral therapy in persons with HIV infection. *Journal of Acquired Immune Deficiency Syndromes, 28,* 445–449.

Anderson, R. J., Freedland, K. E., Clouse, R. E., & Lustman, P. J. (2001). The prevalence of comorbid depression in adults with diabetes: A meta-analysis. *Diabetes Care, 24,* 1069–1078.

Anderson, R. M. (1995). Patient empowerment and the traditional medical model: A case of irreconcilable differences? *Diabetes Care, 18,* 412–415.

Antoni, M. H., Cruess, D. G., Klimas, N., Carrico, A. W., Maher, K., Cruess, S., et al. (2005). Increases in a marker of immune system reconstitution are predated by decreases in 24-h urinary cortisol output and depressed mood during a 10-week stress management intervention in symptomatic HIV-infected men. *Journal of Psychosomatic Research, 58,* 3–13.

Bangsberg, D. R. (2006). Less than 95% adherence to nonnucleoside reverse-transcriptase inhibitor therapy can lead to viral suppression. *Clinical Infectious Diseases, 43,* 939–941.

Beck, A. (1987). *Cognitive therapy of depression.* New York: Guilford Press.

Beck, A. T., Ward, C. H., Mendelson, M., Mock, J., & Erbaugh, J. (1961). An inventory for measuring depression. *Archives of General Psychiatry, 4,* 561–571.

Beck, J. S. (1995). *Cognitive therapy: Basics and beyond.* New York: Guilford Press.

Beck, J., & Beck, A. (1995). *Cognitive therapy.* New York: Guilford Press.

Bedell, C. H. (2003). A changing paradigm for cancer treatment: The advent of new oral chemotherapy agents. *Clinical Journal of Oncology Nursing, 7,* 5–9.

Bedell, C. H., Hartigan, K. J., Wilkinson, K. I., & Halpern, I. M. (2002). Oral chemotherapy: Progress with challenges. *Hematology Oncology News and Issues, 1,* 28–32.

Berenson, G. S., Srinivasan, S. R., Bao, W., Newman, W. P., Tracy, R. E., & Wattigney, W. A. (1998). Association between multiple cardiovascular risk factors and atherosclerosis in children and young adults. *New England Journal of Medicine, 338,* 1650–1656.

Birner, A. (2003). Safe administration of oral chemotherapy. *Clinical Journal of Oncology Nursing, 7,* 1–5.

Blackburn, I. M., Eunson, K. M., & Bishop, S. (1986). A two-year naturalistic follow-up of depressed patients treated with cognitive therapy, pharmacotherapy, and combination of both. *Journal of Affective Disorders, 10,* 67–75.

Bonaccorso, S., Marino, V., Biondi, M., Grimaldi, F., Ippoliti, F., & Maes, M. (2002). Depression induced by treatment with interferon-alpha in patient affected by hepatitis C virus. *Journal of Affective Disorders, 72,* 237–241.

Bruce, D. G., Davis, W. A., & Davis, T. M. (2005). Longitudinal predictors of reduced mobility and physical disability in patients with type 2 diabetes: The Fremantle Diabetes Study. *Diabetes Care, 28,* 2441–2447.

Burns, D. D. (1980). *Feeling good: The new mood therapy.* New York: William Morrow.

Carpenter, C. J., Fischl, M. A., Hammer, S. M., Hirsch, M. S., Jacobsen, D. M., Katzenstein, D. A., et al. (1997). Antiretroviral therapy for HIV infection in 1997: Updated recommendations of the international AIDS society—USA panel. *Journal of the American Medical Association, 277,* 1962–1969.

Casado, J. L., Perez-Elias, M. J., Antela, A., Sabido, R., Marti-Belda, P., Dronda, F., et al. (1998). Predictors of long-term response to protease inhibitor therapy in a cohort of HIV-infected patients. *AIDS, 12,* 131–135.

Chesney, M. A., Ickovics, J. R., Chambers, D. B., Gifford, A. L., Neidig, J., Zwickl, B., et al. (2000). Self-reported adherence to antiretroviral medications among participants in HIV clinical trials: The AACTG adherence instruments. *AIDS Care, 12,* 255–266.

Chesney, M. A., Morin, M., & Sherr, L. (2000). Adherence to HIV combination therapy. *Social Science and Medicine, 50,* 1599–1605.

Cotanch, P. H. (1983). Relaxation training for control of nausea and vomiting in patients receiving chemotherapy. *Cancer Nursing, 6,* 277–283.

Craske, M., Barlow, D. H., & O'Leary, T. A. (1992). *Mastery of your anxiety and worry: Client workbook.* San Antonio, TX: Psychological Corporation.

Cuijpers, P., & Schoevers, R. A. (2004). Increased mortality in depressive disorders: A review. *Current Psychiatry Reports, 6,* 430–437.

Deckersbach, T., Gershuny, B. S., & Otto, M. W. (2000). Cognitive-behavioral therapy for depression: Applications and outcome. *Psychiatric Clinics of North America, 23,* 795–809.

Dew, M. A., Becker, J. T., Sanchez, J., Cladararo, R., Lopez, O. L., Wess, J., et al. (1997). Prevalence and predictors of depressive, anxiety, and substance use disorders in HIV-infected and uninfected men: A longitudinal evaluation. *Psychological Medicine, 27,* 395–409.

Diabetes Control and Complications Trial Research Group. (1993). The effect of intensive treatment of diabetes on the development and progression of long-term complications in insulin-dependent diabetes mellitus. *New England Journal of Medicine, 329,* 977–986.

Dieperink, E., Ho, S. B., Thuras, P., & Willenbring, M. L. (2003). A prospective study of neuropsychiatric symptoms associated with interferon-alpha-2b and ribavirin therapy for patients with chronic hepatitis C. *Psychosomatics, 44,* 104–112.

DiMatteo, M. R., Lepper, H. S., & Croghan, T. W. (2000). Depression is a risk factor for noncompliance with medical treatment: Meta-analysis of the effects of anxiety and depression on patient adherence. *Archives of Internal Medicine, 160,* 2101–2107.

Dobson, K. S. (1989). A meta-analysis of the efficacy of cognitive therapy for depression. *Journal of Consulting and Clinical Psychology, 57,* 414–419.

D'Zurilla, T. J. (1986). *Problem solving therapy: A social competence approach to clinical interventions.* New York: Springer.

Egede, L. E. (2004). Diabetes, major depression, and functional disability among U.S. adults. *Diabetes Care, 27,* 421–428.

Egede, L. E., Zheng, D., & Simpson, K. (2002). Comorbid depression is associated with increased health care use and expenditures in individuals with diabetes. *Diabetes Care, 25,* 464–470.

El Serag, H. B., Kunik, M., Richardson, P., & Rabeneck, L. (2002). Psychiatric disorders among veterans with hepatitis C infection. *Gastroenterology, 123,* 476–482.

Evans, M. D., Hollon, S. D., DeRubeis, R. J., Piasecki, J. M., Grove, W. M., Garvey, M. J., et al. (1992). Differential relapse following cognitive therapy and pharmacotherapy for depression. *Archives of General Psychiatry, 155,* 1443–1445.

Ezzati, M., Lopez, A., Rodgers, A., Vander Hoorn, S., & Murray, C. (2002). Selected major risk factors and global and regional burden of disease. *Lancet, 360,* 1347–1360.

Fätkenheuer, G., Theisen, A., Rockstroh, J., Grabow, T., Wicke, C., Becker, K., et al. (1997). Virological treatment failure of protease inhibitor therapy in an unselected cohort of HIV-infected patients. *AIDS, 11,* 113–116.

Fava, G. A., Grandi, S., Zielezny, M., Canestrari, R., et al. (1995). Cognitive-behavioral treatment of residual symptoms in primary major depressive disorder. *American Journal of Psychiatry, 151,* 1295–1299.

Fava, G. A., Grandi, S., Zielezny, M., Rafanelli, C., et al. (1996). Four-year outcome for cognitive-behavioral treatment of residual symptoms in major depression. *American Journal of Psychiatry, 153,* 945–947.

Fava, G. A., Rafanelli, C., Grandi, S., Canestrari, R., & Morphy, M. A. (1998). Six-year outcome for cognitive behavioral treatment of residual symptoms in major depression. *American Journal of Psychiatry, 155,* 1443–1445.

Fava, G. A., Rafanelli, C., Grandi, S., Conti, S., & Belluardo, P. (1998). Prevention of recurrent depression with cognitive behavioral therapy. *Archives of General Psychiatry, 55,* 816–820.

Fava, M., Alpert, J. E., Nierenberg, A. A., Worthington, J. J., & Rosenbaum, J. F. (2000, May). *Double-blind study of high dose fluoxetine versus lithium or desipramine augmentation of fluoxetine in partial and non-responders to fluoxetine.* Paper presented at the annual meeting of the American Psychiatric Association, Chicago.

Fava, M., & Davidson, K. G. (1996) Definition and epidemiology of treatment-resistant depression. *Psychiatric Clinics of North America, 19,* 179–200.

Fields, L. E., Burt, V. L., Cutler, J. A., Hughes, J., Roccella, E. J., & Sorlie, P. (2004). The burden of adult hypertension in the United States from 1999–2000: A rising tide. *Hypertension, 44,* 398–404.

Fisher, J. D., & Fisher, W. A. (1992). Changing AIDS risk behavior. *Psychological Bulletin, 111,* 455–474.

Frasure-Smith, N., Lesperance, F., & Talajic, M. (1993). Depression following myocardial infarction: Impact on 6-month survival. *Journal of the American Medical Association, 270,* 1819–1825.

Frasure-Smith, N., Lesperance, F., & Talajic, M. (1995a). Depression and 18-month prognosis after myocardial infarction. *Circulation, 91,* 999–1005.

Frasure-Smith, N., Lesperance, F., & Talajic, M. (1995b). The impact of negative emotions on prognosis following myocardial infarction: Is it more than depression? *Health Psychology, 14,* 388–398.

Gleason, O., Yates, W., Isbell, M. D., & Phillipsen, M. A. (2002). An open-label trial of citalopram for major depression in patients with hepatitis C. *Journal of Clinical Psychiatry, 63,* 194–198.

Goldney, R. D., Phillips, P. J., Fisher, L. J., & Wilson, D. H. (2004). Diabetes, depression, and quality of life: A population study. *Diabetes Care, 27,* 1066–1070.

Gonzalez, J. S., Penedo, F. J., Antoni, M. H., Duran, R. E., Fernandez, M. I., McPherson-Baker, S., et al. (2004). Social support, positive states of mind, and HIV treatment adherence in men and women living with HIV/AIDS. *Health Psychology, 23,* 413–418.

Gonzalez, J. S., Safren, S. A., Cagliero, E., Wexler, D. J., Delahanty, L., Wittenberg, E., et al. (in press). Clinical and sub-clinical depression, self-care, and medication adherence in type 2 diabetes. *Diabetes Care.*

Goodwin, J. S., Zhang, D. D., & Ostir, G. V. (2004). Effect of depression on diagnosis, treatment, and survival of older women with breast cancer. *Journal of the American Geriatrics Society, 52,* 106–111.

Halm, E. A., Mora, P., & Leventhal, H. (2006). The acute episodic disease belief is associated with poor self-management among inner-city adults with persistent asthma. *Chest, 129,* 573–580.

Hauser, P., Khosla, J., Aurora, H., Laurin, J., Kling, M. A., Hill, J., et al. (2002). A prospective study of the incidence and open-label treatment of interferon-induced major depressive disorder in patients with hepatitis C. *Molecular Psychiatry, 7*, 942–947.

Heimberg, R. G. (1991). *Cognitive-behavioral therapy of social phobia in a group setting.* Unpublished ms.

Hickling, E. J., & Blanchard, E. B. (2006). *Overcoming the trauma of your motor vehicle accident: A cognitive-behavioral treatment program workbook.* New York: Oxford University Press.

Holmes, V., & Griffiths, P. (2002). Self-monitoring of glucose levels for people with type 2 diabetes. *British Journal of Community Nursing, 7*, 41–46.

Hope, D. A., Heimberg, R. G., Juster, H. R., & Turk, C. L. (2000). *Managing social anxiety: A cognitive-behavioral therapy approach.* Boulder, CO: Greywind.

Horwitz, R. I., Viscoli, C. M., Berkman, L., Donaldson, R. M., Horwitz, S. M., Murray, C. J., et al. (1990). Treatment adherence and risk of death after a myocardial infarction. *Lancet, 336,* 542–545.

Januzzi, J. L., Stern, T. A., Pasternak, R. C., & DeSantis, R. W. (2000). The influence of anxiety and depression on outcomes of patients with coronary artery disease. *Archives of Internal Medicine, 160,* 1913–1921.

Jonas, B. S., Franks, P., & Ingram, D. D. (1997). Are symptoms of anxiety and depression risk factors for hypertension? Longitudinal evidence from the National Health and Nutrition Examination Survey I Epidemiologic Follow-Up Study. *Archives of Family Medicine, 6,* 43–49.

Karter, A. J. (2001). Self-monitoring of blood glucose levels and glycemic control: The Northern California Kaiser Permanente diabetes registry. *American Journal of Medicine, 111,* 1–9.

Katon, W. J., & Ciechanowski, P. (2002). Impact of major depression on chronic medical illness. *Journal of Psychosomatic Research, 53,* 859–863.

Katon, W. J., Rutter, C., Simon, G., Lin, E. H., Ludman, E., Ciechanowski, P., et al. (2005). The association of comorbid depression with mortality in patients with type 2 diabetes. *Diabetes Care, 28,* 2668–2670.

Katon, W. J., Simon, G., Russo, J., Von Korff, M., Lin, E. H., Ludman, E., et al. (2004). Quality of depression care in a population-based sample of patients with diabetes and major depression. *Medical Care, 42,* 1222–1229.

Katon, W. J., & Sullivan, M. D. (1990). Depression and chronic medical illness. *Juvenile Clinical Psychiatry, 51,* 3–14.

Kearney, P., Whelton, M., Reynolds, K., Muntner, P., & Whelton, J. (2005). Global burden of hypertension: Analysis of worldwide data. *Lancet, 365,* 217–223.

Kim, W. R. (2002). The burden of hepatitis C in the United States. *Hepatology, 36,* S30-S34.

Knott, A., Dieperink, E., Willenbring, M. L., Heit, S., Durfee, J. M., Wingert, M., et al. (2006). Integrated psychiatric/medical care in a chronic hepatitis C clinic: Effect on antiviral treatment evaluation and outcomes. *American Journal of Gastroenterology, 101,* 2254–2262.

Kraus, M. R., Schafer, A., Csef, H., Scheurlen, M., & Faller, H. (2000). Emotional state, coping styles, and somatic variables in patients with chronic hepatitis C. *Psychosomatics, 41,* 377–378.

Ladwig, K., Kieser, M., König, J., Breithardt, G., & Borggrefe, M. (1991). Affective disorders and survival after acute MI. *European Heart Journal, 12,* 959–964.

Lavoie, K. L., Bacon, S. L., Barone, S., Cartier, A., Ditto, B., & Labrecque, M. (2006). What is worse for asthma control and quality of life: Depressive disorders, anxiety disorders, or both? *Chest, 130,* 1039–1047.

Lebovits, A. H., Strain, J. J., Schleifer, S. J., Tanaka, J. S., Bhardwaj, S., & Messe, M. R. (1990). Patient noncompliance with self-administered chemotherapy. *Cancer, 65,* 17–22.

Lett, H. S., Blumenthal, J. A., Babyak, M. A., Sherwood, A., Strauman, T., Robins, C., et al. (2004). Depression as a risk factor for coronary artery disease: Evidence, mechanisms, and treatment. *Psychosomatic Medicine, 66,* 305–315.

Linehan, M. (1993). *Skills training manual for treating borderline personality disorder.* New York: Guilford Press.

Lustman, P. J., Griffith, L. S., Freedland, K. E., Kissel, S. S., & Clouse, R. E. (1998). Cognitive behavior therapy for depression in type 2 diabetes mellitus. *Annals of Internal Medicine, 129,* 613–621.

Mannino, D. M., Homa, D. M., Akinbami, L. J., Ford, E. S., & Redd, S. C. (2002). Chronic obstructive pulmonary disease surveillance—United States, 1971–2000. *Morbidity and Mortality Weekly Report, 51,* 1–16.

McDermott, M. M., Schmitt, B., & Walner, E. (1997). Impact of medication nonadherence on coronary heart disease outcomes: A critical review. *Archives of Internal Medicine, 157,* 1921–1929.

McLean, P. D., & Hakstian, A. R. (1990). Relative endurance of unipolar depression treatment effects: Longitudinal follow-up. *Journal of Consulting and Clinical Psychology, 58,* 482–488.

Miller, W. R., & Rollnick, S. (1991). *Motivational interviewing: Preparing people to change addictive behavior.* New York: Guilford Press.

Morris, P. L., Robinson, R. G., Andrzejewski, P., Samuels, J., & Price, T. R. (1993). Association of depression with 10-year poststroke mortality. *American Juvenile Psychiatry, 150,* 124–129.

Nathan, D. M. (1996). The pathophysiology of diabetic complications: How much does the glucose hypothesis explain? *Annals of Internal Medicine, 124,* 86–89.

National Institute of Mental Health. (1985). CGI: Clinical Global Impression Scale—NIMH. *Psychopharmacology Bulletin, 21,* 839–844.

Nezu, A. M., Nezu, C. M., Friedman, S. H., Faddis, S., & Houts, P. S. (1998). *Helping cancer patients cope: A problem-solving approach.* Washington, DC: American Psychological Association.

Nezu, A. M., Nezu, C. M., Friedman, S. H., Houts, P. S., & Faddis, S. (1997). Project Genesis. Unpublished application.

Nezu, A. M., & Perri, M. G. (1989). Social problem-solving therapy for unipolar depression: An initial dismantling investigation. *Journal of Consulting and Clinical Psychology, 57,* 408–413.

Ohkubo, Y., Hiskikawa, H., Araki, E., Miyata, T., Isami, S., Motoyoshi, S., et al. (1995). Intensive insulin therapy prevents the progression of diabetic microvascular complications in Japanese patients with non-insulin-dependent diabetes mellitus: A randomized prospective 6-year study. *Diabetes Research and Clinical Practice, 28,* 103–117.

Olatunji, B. O, Mimiaga, M. J., O'Clereigh, C., & Safren, S. A. (2006). Review of treatment studies of depression in HIV. *Topics in HIV Medicine, 14,* 112–124.

Ost, L. (n.d.). *Applied relaxation: Manual for a behavioral coping technique.* Unpublished manuscript, Stockholm University.

Otto, M. (2000). Stories and metaphors in cognitive-behavior therapy. *Cognitive and Behavioral Practice, 7,* 166–172.

Otto, M., Reilly-Harrington, N., Kogan, J. L., Henin, A., & Knauz, R. O. (2000). *Treatment of bipolar disorder: A cognitive-behavioral manual.* Unpublished manuscript.

Otto, M. W., Jones, J. C., Craske, M. G., & Barlow, D. H. (1996). *Stopping anxiety medication: Panic control therapy for benzodiazepine discontinuation. Therapist guide.* San Antonio, TX: Psychological Corporation.

Otto, M. W., Pava, J., & Sprich-Buckminster, S. (1996). Treatment of major depression: Application and efficacy of cognitive-behavioral therapy. In M. H. Pollack, M. W. Otto, & J. F. Rosenbaum (Eds.), *Challenges in clinical practice: Pharmacologic and psychosocial strategies.* New York: Guilford Press.

Paterson, D. L., Swindells, S., Mohr, J., Vergis, E. N., Squire, C., Wagener, M. M., et al. (2000). Adherence to protease inhibitor therapy and outcomes in patients with HIV infection. *Annals of Internal Medicine, 133,* 21–30.

Paykel, E. S., Scott, J., Teasdale, J. D., Johnson, A. L., Garland, A., Moore, R., et al. (1999). Prevention of relapse in residual depression by cognitive therapy: A controlled trial. *Archives of General Psychiatry, 56,* 829–835.

Persons, J. (1989). *Cognitive therapy in practice: A case formulation approach.* New York: Norton.

Perz, J. F., Farrington, L. A., & Pecoraro, C. (2004, September–October). *Estimated global prevalence of hepatitis C virus infection.* Paper presented at the annual meeting of the Infectious Diseases Society of America, Boston.

Piette, J. D., Heisler, M., & Wagner, T. H. (2004). Problems paying out-of-pocket medication costs among older adults with diabetes. *Diabetes Care, 27,* 384–391.

Pirl, W. F., & Roth, A. J. (1999). Diagnosis and treatment of depression in cancer patients. *Oncology, 13,* 1293–1301.

Rabkin, J. G. (1996). Prevalence of psychiatric disorders in HIV illness. *International Review of Psychiatry, 8,* 157–166.

Reichard, P., Nilsson, B. Y., & Rosenqvist, V. (1993). The effect of long-term intensified insulin treatment on the development of microvascular complications of diabetes mellitus. *New England Journal of Medicine, 329,* 304–309.

Rieckmann, N., Gerin, W., Kronish, I. M., Burg, M. M., Chaplin, W. F., Kong, G., et al. (2006). Course of depressive symptoms and medication adherence after acute coronary syndromes. *Journal of American College of Cardiology, 48,* 2218–2222.

Robinson, L. A., Berman, J. S., & Neimeyer, R. A. (1990). Psychotherapy for the treatment of depression: A comprehensive review of controlled outcome research. *Psychological Bulletin, 108,* 30–49.

Rodin, G. M., Nolan, R. P., & Katz, M. R. (2005). Depression. In J. L. Levenson (Ed.), *Textbook of psychosomatic medicine* (pp. 193–217). Washington, DC: American Psychiatric..

Rubin, R. R. (2005). Adherence to pharmacologic therapy in patients with type 2 diabetes mellitus. *The American Journal of Medicine, 118,* 27S–34S.

Rubin, R. R., & Peyrot, M. (1999). Quality of life and diabetes. *Diabetes Metabolic Research Review, 15,* 205–218.

Rubin, R. R., & Peyrot, M. (2001). Psychological issues and treatments for people with diabetes. *Journal of Clinical Psychology, 57,* 457–478.

Sadock, B. J., & Sadock, V. A. (2003). *Kaplan and Sadock's Synopsis of psychiatry: Behavioral sciences/clinical psychiatry* (9th ed.). New York: Lippincott Williams & Wilkins.

Safren, S. A., Hendriksen, E. S., Mayer, K. H., Mimiaga, M. J., Pickard, R., & Otto, M. W. (2004). Cognitive behavioral therapy for HIV medication adherence and depression. *Cognitive and Behavioral Practice, 11,* 415–423.

Safren, S. A., Knauz, R. O., O'Cleirigh, C., Lerner, J., Greer, J., Harwood, M., Tan, J., & Mayer, K. H. (2006, March). CBT for HIV medication adherence and depression: Process and outcome at posttreatment and three-month crossover. Paper presented as part of a symposium at the annual meeting of the Society of Behavioral Medicine, San Francisco, CA.

Safren, S. A., Otto, M. W., & Worth, J. (1999). Life-steps: Applying cognitive-behavioral therapy to patient adherence to HIV medication treatment. *Cognitive and Behavioral Practice, 6,* 332–341.

Safren, S. A., Otto, M. W., Worth, J., Salomon, E., Johnson, W., Mayer, K., et al. (2001). Two strategies to increase adherence to HIV antiretroviral medication: Life-steps and medication monitoring. *Behavioural Research and Therapy, 39,* 1151–1162.

Schectman, J. M., Nadkarni, M. M., & Voss, J. D. (2002). The association between diabetes metabolic control and drug adherence in an indigent population. *Diabetes Care, 25,* 15–21.

Schleifer, S. J., Macara-Hinson, M. M., Coyle, D. A., Slater, W. R., Kahn, M., Gorlin, R., et al. (1989). The nature and course of depression following myocardial infarction. *Archives of Internal Medicine, 149,* 1785–1789.

Silverstone, P. H. (1990). Changes in depression scores following life-threatening illness. *Journal of Psychosomatic Research, 34,* 659–663.

Simoni, J. M., Frick, P. A., Lockhart, D., & Liebovitz, D. (2002). Mediators of social support and antiretroviral adherence among an indigent population in New York City. *AIDS Patient Care and STDs, 16,* 431–439.

Simons, A. D., Murphy, G. E., Levine, J. L., & Wetzel, R. D. (1986). Cognitive therapy and pharmacotherapy for depression: Sustained improvement over one year. *Archives of General Psychiatry, 43,* 43–48.

Singh, N., Squier, C., Sivek, C., Wagener, M., Nguyen, M. H., & Yu, V. L. (1996). Determinants of compliance with antiretroviral therapy in patients with human immunodeficiency virus: Prospective assessment with implications for enhancing compliance. *AIDS Care, 10,* 1033–1039.

Smith, A., Krishnan, J. A., Bilderback, A., Reikert, K. A., Rand, C. S., & Bartlett, S. J. (2006). Depressive symptoms and adherence to asthma therapy after hospital discharge. *Chest, 130,* 1034–1038.

Smith, W. B. (1987). Biofeedback and relaxation training: The effect on headache and associated symptoms. *Headache, 27,* 511–514.

Soroudi, N., Perez, G. K., Pollack, M. H., Otto, M. W., Gonzalez, J. S., Greer, J. A., et al. (in press). CBT for adherence and depression (CBT-AD) in HIV-infected methadone patients. *Cognitive and Behavioral Practice.*

Spiegel, D., & Giese-Davis, J. (2003). Depression and cancer: Mechanisms and disease progression. *Biological Psychiatry, 54,* 269–282.

Strader, D. B., Wright, T., Thomas, D. L., & Seeff, L. B. (2004). AASLD practice guideline: Diagnosis, management, and treatment of hepatitis C. *Hepatology, 39,* 1147–1171.

Teasdale, J. D., Segal, Z. V., Williams, J. M., Ridgeway, V. A., Soulsby, J. M., & Lau, M. A. (2000). Prevention of relapse/recurrence in major depression by mindfulness-based cognitive therapy. *Journal of Consulting and Clinical Psychology, 68,* 615–623.

Turner, J. A., & Chapman, C. R. (1982). Psychological interventions for chronic pain: A critical review. I. Relaxation and biofeedback. *Pain, 12,* 1–21.

Turner, R., Cull, C., & Holman, R. (1996). United Kingdom Prospective Diabetes Study 17: A 9-year update of a randomized, controlled trial on the effect of improved metabolic control on complications in non-insulin-dependent diabetes mellitus. *Annals of Internal Medicine, 124,* 136–145.

Valente, S. M., Saunders, J. M., & Cohen, M. Z. (1994). Evaluating depression among patients with cancer. *Cancer Practice, 2,* 67–71.

Van Melle, J. P., de Jonge, P., Spijkerman, T. A., Tijssen, J. G. P., Ormel, J., van Veldhuisen, D. J., et al. (2004). Prognostic association of depression following myocardial infarction with mortality and cardiovascular events: A meta-analysis. *Psychosomatic Medicine, 66,* 814–822.

Wang, P. S., Bohn, R. L., Knight, E., Glynn, R. J., Mogun, H., & Avorn, J. (2002). Noncompliance with antihypertensive medications: The impact of depressive symptoms and psychosocial factors. *Journal of General Internal Medicine, 17,* 504–511.

Waterhouse, D. M., Calzone, K. A., Mele, C., & Brenner, D. E. (1993). Adherence to oral tamoxifen: A comparison of patient self-report, pill counts, and microelectronic monitoring. *Journal of Clinical Oncology, 11,* 2457–2458.

Weiss, K., & Sullivan, S. (2001). The health economics of asthma and rhinitis: I. Assessing the economic impact? *Journal of Allergy and Clinical Immunology, 107,* 3–8.

Weissman, M. M. (2005). *Mastering depression through interpersonal psychotherapy: Patient workbook.* New York: Oxford University Press.

Wells, K. B., Rogers, W., Burnam, A., Greenfield, S., & Ware, J. E., Jr. (1991). How the medical comorbidity of depressed patients differs across health care settings: Results from the Medical Outcomes Study. *American Juvenile Psychiatry, 148,* 1688–1696.

Williams, J. W., Katon, W., Lin, E. H., Noel, P. H., Worchel, J., Cornell, J., et al. (2004). The effectiveness of depression care management on diabetes-related outcomes in older patients. *Annals of Internal Medicine, 140,* 1015–1024.

Ziegelstein, R. C., Fauerbach, J. A., Stevens, S. S., Romanelli, J., Richter, D. P., & Bush, D. E. (2000). Patients with depression are less likely to follow recommendations to reduce cardiac risk during recovery from a myocardial infarction. *Archives of Internal Medicine, 160,* 1818–1823.

About the Authors

Dr. Steven Safren is an Associate Professor in Psychology at Harvard Medical School and the Director of Behavioral Medicine in the Department of Psychiatry at Massachusetts General Hospital (MGH). He also directs the cognitive-behavioral track and behavioral medicine training tracks of the MGH clinical psychology internship and is a research scientist at Fenway Community Health. Dr. Safren received his PhD in clinical psychology from the University at Albany, State University of New York, in 1998 and did his internship and postdoctoral fellowship at Massachusetts General Hospital/Harvard Medical School. Dr. Safren has over 75 professional publications. He has received several grants from the National Institutes of Health (NIH) to develop and evaluate cognitive-behavioral interventions, including two studies of CBT-AD in patients with HIV and depression and one in patients with diabetes and depression. Additional NIH funding includes studies of CBT for adults with ADHD. Dr. Safren has served as a regular reviewer for the National Institutes of Health's study section, which reviews grants related to behavioral aspects of HIV/AIDS.

Dr. Jeffrey S. Gonzalez is a Clinical Assistant in Psychology at Massachusetts General Hospital and an Instructor in Psychology at Harvard Medical School. Dr. Gonzalez received his PhD in clinical psychology, with a specialization in health psychology, from the University of Miami. He completed his internship and postdoctoral fellowship at Massachusetts General Hospital/Harvard Medical School. In 2006 he was awarded the Early Career Award by the International Society of Behavioral Medicine. Dr. Gonzalez has 20 professional publications on behavioral medicine approaches to the study of HIV, diabetes, and cancer. He is currently co-principal investigator and project director on an NIH-funded grant to evaluate the efficacy of CBT-AD in patients with diabetes and depression. He is also a protocol therapist on both this study and a trial of CBT-AD in patients with depression and HIV. Dr. Gonzalez is a licensed psychologist specializing in behavioral medicine interventions for clients with chronic medical conditions and cognitive-behavioral therapy approaches to the treatment of mood and anxiety disorders.

Dr. Nafisseh Soroudi is a Clinical Fellow in Psychiatry at Massachusetts General Hospital (MGH). Dr. Soroudi received her PhD in clinical health psychology from Yeshiva University, Ferkauf Graduate School of Psychology. She completed her internship at Montefiore Medical Center and her postdoctoral fellowship at Massachusetts General Hospital/Harvard Medical School. Dr. Soroudi has several professional publications on behavioral medicine approaches to the study of HIV, obesity, and diabetes. She is currently the project director and a protocol therapist of a NIDA-funded grant to evaluate the efficacy of CBT-AD in patients with HIV and on methadone therapy. Clinically, Dr. Soroudi specializes in behavioral medicine interventions for clients and couples with chronic medical conditions and cognitive-behavioral therapy approaches to the treatment of mood and anxiety disorders.

Authors' note: This treatment was developed as part of several NIH grants awarded to Dr. Safren and colleagues. These include grants MH066660 (Safren), MH078571 (Safren and Gonzalez) from the National Institute of Mental Health, and grant DA018603 (Safren) from the National Institute of Drug Abuse.